BETWEEN THE WOODS AND THE CRICK

Between the Woods and the Crick

By Jean L. DeLong

LIFESTORY PUBLISHING ORLANDO, FLORIDA

LifeStory Publishing
P. O. Box 541527
Orlando, FL 32854

ISBN 13: 978-1-939472-06-9
ISBN 10: 1939472067

PRINTED IN THE UNITED STATES OF AMERICA

COVER AND INTERIOR DESIGN BY ALBERT CHIANG/SURFVIEWDNA.COM

FIRST EDITION: MARCH 2013
10 9 8 7 6 5 4 3 2 1

Dedication

To my children and grandchildren

with much love

Table of Contents

Acknowledgments

FIRST AND FOREMOST, for my friend, author Harriette Cole of Harriette Cole Media who gave me the courage to write my stories. For that, I'm forever grateful.

FOR MY LIFELONG FRIENDS—Gayle McCormick, Patti Bonadio and Bette Gerardi—and my school friends—Janet Carlson, Sherri Smith and Norma Ellberg—who helped my stories become a book.

FOR MY LOVING FAMILY who spurred me on for three years.

FOR PATRICIA CHARPENTIER, my editor who had the patience, endurance, and kindness I needed to carry me through.

FOR MY PARENTS who allowed me to be curious, adventurous, strong, and independent. That gift helped me through the rough times in my life.

AND FOR MY PARTNER IN LIFE, Bob Wieseneck, who helped me with the technical aspects of the book and encouraged me when I felt insecure. I couldn't have done it without you. You are a saint!

Prologue

AS I AGED, I've felt a great need to write a book about my younger days. I was fortunate to have parents who encouraged my curiosity and gave me the freedom to explore and discover what a big world we live in. I woke up every morning, rain or shine, excited about what might be waiting for me around the corner. Those years were the best times of my life, filled with lots of adventures, which created in me the resilience for dealing with tougher issues as I grew up.

I met Patricia Charpentier several years ago when a friend and I went to a book fair in Vero Beach, which featured author Mike Leonard, feature writer for NBC's *Today* show at the time. I especially wanted a copy of Mike's book, *The Ride of Our Lives*. My friend and I talked with Mike as he signed my book, and I asked if he knew of any ghostwriters. Sadly he did not, so we thanked him and walked on down the street.

Halfway down the block, I heard the sound of running feet behind me and turned to see Mike sprinting toward us. Out of breath, he exclaimed that he had just met a ghostwriter, and she was still at his booth. We walked back with him and met Patricia Charpentier. She was businesslike, articulate and friendly and gave me her card to get in touch with her about helping me write my book. I tucked her card away and later put it in a folder at home for safekeeping.

Time passed and the card was forgotten, but the dream of writing a book was not. *One day, one day I'll do it*, I kept telling myself. A year or so later while organizing my art and photo files, a little card floated out of a folder and fell to the floor. That was the sign I needed; it was time to write my book with Patricia's help.

Now, three years later, *Between the Woods and the Crick* is finished and off my mind. *I did it!* Turn the page and travel back with me to the 1930s and 1940s in Warren, Pennsylvania, and relive sunny days filled with friends, exploration, imagination, and adventure.

Curious Jean

I HAD AN UNEVENTFUL BIRTH, according to my mother, but it wasn't uneventful for me. Saturday, July 6, 1935 was a great day. I weighed in at six pounds and some ounces, ready for all that life had to offer. On that same day on the other side of the world, Tibet's fourteenth Dalai Lama was born, destined for greatness, but other than that, the calendar of significant events for the year 1935 doesn't even have one entry for July.

Our family started without me, so I had a lot of catching up to do. My brother Donnie was one and a half years old when I was born, and my sister Kaye was two years older than Donnie.

Mom told me I walked when I was nine months old; I had places to go and crawling just didn't get me there fast enough. By the time I was two, we lived on Brook Street, and Mom said she could not keep track of me. In desperation one day, she took some

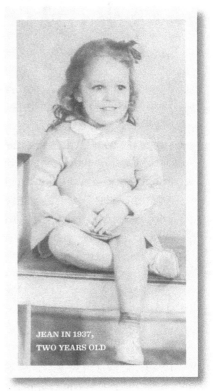

JEAN IN 1937,
TWO YEARS OLD

clothesline and tied one end to the front porch railing and the other to the back straps of my sun suit. She felt certain this would keep me from wandering off, so she could get her housework done.

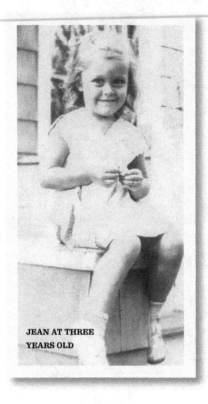

JEAN AT THREE YEARS OLD

Mom was deep into her chores an hour later when someone knocked at the front door. When she answered it, she was shocked to see our neighbor holding me in his arms in my *altogether*. He explained that as he walked down the street to his house about a block away, he saw me running toward him without a stitch of clothes on, wearing only a gleeful look on my face. He scooped me up into his arms and carried me home. My mom laughed, thanked him and knew that she'd have to come up with a more sophisticated way to keep me where I belonged. She said that I was like a little monkey— small enough to walk under tables, able to climb as well as I could walk and impossible to keep track of.

WHEN I TURNED THREE, we moved to Connecticut Avenue and lived in a white, two-story house on a hill. One night I fell out of bed and broke my collarbone and had to keep my arm in a sling so it could heal. Somebody was *supposed* to be watching me while Mom went to the grocery store, but apparently they weren't as diligent as they should have been. I hopped on my tricycle and started down the hill, which was approximately one block long.

Mom pulled up just in time to see me going lickety-split down the sidewalk with one arm in the sling, my legs sticking straight out at the sides, a huge grin covering my face and the pedals of my tricycle spinning like a top. She held her breath until I reached the bottom of the hill and knew I was safe. Then she proceeded to warm my butt and took my trike away for three days.

MOM AND DADDY HAD A FRIEND, Millie Anderson, who occasionally came to visit when we lived on Connecticut Avenue. Millie was a heavy smoker and lit up one cigarette after another the entire time she was at our house. Her process fascinated me. She took a cigarette out of the special container she had for them and gently tamped it against the smooth, metal case. This packed down the tobacco, so she didn't get loose bits in her mouth. Once in a while, her method didn't work, so she stuck her tongue out just a little and wiped the tiny piece of tobacco off with her middle finger. Then she gently

JEAN, DONNIE AND KAYE (FRONT) BILL, JR. AND NEIGHBOR GIRLS (BACK) WITH PUPPIES
IN THE SIMONSENS' BACKYARD

held the cigarette between her index and middle fingers and eased it up to her mouth every few seconds. With her brightly colored lips barely touching the cigarette, she sucked air through the white stick, making her cheeks sink in just a little while the end of the cigarette burned brighter. Then she turned up her head a tad and blew the smoke into the air. Quite often, she flicked the ashes into the ashtray, so they wouldn't fall on the floor. This was a great show for me to watch.

One day when Mom and Millie stepped into the kitchen, I picked up the cigarette she left in the ashtray and tried to imitate what she did. I took in a mouthful of smoke and began to cough. I coughed and coughed until Mom finally came in and caught me in the act. After she ripped the cigarette out of my mouth, another butt warming followed.

GETTING SPANKED was nothing out of the ordinary for me growing up; I got paddled every day for one thing or another. If a day went by that I didn't get smacked, I wondered what was wrong.

WE HAD A NEXT-DOOR NEIGHBOR named Bill Simonsen who was probably fifty years old and loved to sit out on his front porch and watch the world go by. He was tall and skinny and always used suspenders to hold up his pants.

KAYE, DONNIE AND JEAN, SHOWING OFF THEIR NEW HAIRCUTS

Sometimes he'd call me over, put me on his lap and drop his false teeth down into his hand to watch the expression on my face. I just sat there with my mouth wide open, looking at his big, gummy smile and laughed so hard. It was the funniest thing I had ever seen. "Do it again, Bill. Do it again," I giggled, and he did, over and over and over. I never got enough of watching him do that. He liked it as much as I did. With his rocking chair tipped back, he always threw his head back and laughed and laughed, which made me laugh even more.

NEEDING A LITTLE ENTERTAINMENT once in a while, Mom sometimes took me, my brother Donnie and my sister Kaye to early afternoon movies at the Struthers Library Theatre in Warren. We climbed on the bus at the corner of Kenmore Street and Conewango Avenue and headed for the theatre, getting off at the depot on the corner of Pennsylvania Avenue and Liberty Street.

More exciting to me than the movie was the snack counter. While Mom bought the tickets and Donnie and Kaye got candy or popcorn, I loaded up on Good & Plenty candy. Donnie and Kaye picked something different every time, but I never strayed from my all-time favorite—those little bright pink and white, candy-coated bits of licorice.

The Library Theatre was a beautiful old theatre that Mom said was built in the late 1800s, which meant it was really old, older than Grandma even. It had big, red, plush seats and a balcony that was usually empty on weekday afternoons when we went. We felt special going there, like it was our own personal theatre.

Navigating all of our moods must have been difficult for Mom. I had to have my Good & Plenty candy. If the snack bar was sold out, it wasn't going to be a pleasant afternoon for anyone. When Mom chose to see a *shoot-*

'em-up western or cowboy movie, Donnie was happy. He was ready to leave as soon as any other type of movie began. If it was a sad, romantic movie, Kaye sobbed through the entire film. I didn't care much about the movie as long as I had my Good & Plenty candy. I'd sit through almost anything, content holding that little purple box in my hands.

KAYE, JEAN AND DONNIE - 1940

OUR FAMILY PLUS A COUPLE of my uncles went to Niagara Falls one summer when I was five years old. It was a long trip especially with my short attention span. Within ten minutes, my litany of questions began.

Are we almost there?
When are we going to get there?
Can we stop and get something to eat?
Can we get something to drink?
I got to go to the bathroom.
When are we going to stop?

OUR CAR WAS FULL—Dad; Uncle Don, my mom's brother; and Uncle Chuck, my mom's brother-in-law, in the front seat. Mom, Kaye, Donnie and me in the back seat, and it was *hot*. Donnie sat next to me, and his sweaty skin rubbed against mine as we were all squished together. "Mom, Donnie's touching me," I whined. It was more than I could stand. "Mom, can I have the back window down some more?"

"No Jean. The wind is blowing my hair all over as it is," Mom replied.

Donnie and Kaye took naps and slept the hours away. I stared out the back window, looking for animals to distract myself from the heat and my sweaty brother.

Two hours later, we finally arrived at Niagara Falls and got out of that hot, crowded car. The fresh, misty air cooled us off as we walked down the wooden stairways where we could get closer to the falls. I thought they were beautiful and huge and scary. And loud...we had to yell at each other just to be heard. We watched the *Maid of the Mist*, filled with people in yellow raincoats, trying to keep dry as the boat navigated through the massive rocks and crashing waters. We all *ooh'd* and *ahh'd* for a time and ate our lunch at a picnic table overlooking the falls. Then it was time to get back into the hot car and go home.

Along the way home, Daddy and my uncles decided they were thirsty and stopped at a bar to *wet their whistles*. "Mom, I didn't see any whistles. What kind of whistles do they have? Why can't I play with one of their whistles while we wait in the car?" I asked.

"Jean, there are no whistles. It's just a figure of speech," she said, settling back in her seat and closing her eyes. I didn't know what that was either, but I figured I'd ask about it some other time. We waited and waited until Mom finally got tired of it and sent me into the bar to get the men.

She watched as I walked the short distance to the bar. I opened the door and stepped inside the warm, dimly-lit room that smelled of beer and cigar and cigarette smoke. It took me a minute or so to spot my dad and uncles in the far corner, sitting around a small table with smoke wafting toward the ceiling. Standing in the entrance, I put my hands on my hips and shouted above the many garbled conversations, "Daddy, Mom says she's been in the car with us long enough. It's time to go home!" A burst of laughter filled the room as I turned on my heels and marched out the door. I reported to Mom they would be back soon. A couple of minutes later, the men walked out of the bar, chuckling, got into the car, and we headed home.

ONE TIME WE HAD A LEAK in a water line outside the house, and Dad called someone to fix it. A nice, bearded man in a red-plaid shirt showed up to take care of the problem. Watching him dig was very interesting to me, so while he worked, I plopped down beside him and asked questions.

What are you doing?
Why are you doing that?
Why is the hole so big?
What are you digging for?
How come you have to dig so far?

Do you like to dig?
Do you have any little kids?

AND MY STANDARD QUESTION for everyone I really liked, "When are you leaving?" I asked that because I wanted to know how much time I had left to spend with them. I didn't want him to leave too soon.

Mom had known this man for years, so she didn't have any hesitation in letting me be with him. She was also probably grateful to get me out of her hair for a while.

He stopped to eat his lunch at noon and asked me, "Why don't you bring your lunch out here and eat with me?" Mom made me a peanut butter sandwich, and I raced back to where he was sitting on an upturned bucket under a tree. He told me his name was Joe, and he taught me a little saying,

Hello Joe, whaddya know?
I just got back from Buffalo.

AFTER A COUPLE OF DAYS, Joe's work finally came to an end; the leak was repaired, and he had to go on to another job. I was sad to see him leave, but he told me to remember the little saying and think of him. I still do.

Grandparents

BEATRICE

I AWOKE IN A BIG, SOFT BED, a feather-mattress cocoon, slowly opened my eyes and gazed up at the marble bust of Beatrice—supposedly a goddess or something—glowing in the early morning sunlight. Beatrice sat serenely, watching over me, from the ledge of the round, stained glass window near the ceiling. The figure in the stained glass looked like someone I'd see in heaven, and the various pieces of pink, blue, green and yellow glass bathed Beatrice in a rainbow of soft colors. This was my Aunt Roanie's bedroom in the big house at One Second Avenue in Warren, Pennsylvania. Rosamond Mayme DeLong, Aunt Roanie as I called her, was my father's sister.

This house belonged to my grandparents, Clifton Pratt and Lucile Knapp DeLong, and I was staying here for a few days after my mom gave birth to my sister Linda. This arrangement allowed my mother to have a break and provided me with some concentrated attention, the kind I wasn't likely to get with a new baby in the house. My

DONNIE, AUNT ROANIE, JEAN AND KAYE

**GREAT-GRANDFATHER,
THE HONORABLE FRANK M. KNAPP**

parents and grandparents knew I would no longer enjoy the important role of *baby of the family* that I held for seven years, so they tried to give me a little extra attention before I went back home.

My grandmother inherited this huge, three-story home from my great-grandparents, the Honorable Frank M. and Rosamond Ensworth Knapp. My great-grandfather had been one of the most prominent men in Northwestern Pennsylvania both in business and politics. He even served as state senator from 1910 – 1914. The house was in keeping with my great-grandfather's status in life. Built in the Queen Anne style popular at that time, the house was constructed using yellowish-tan brick, had bay windows, a wrap-around porch, gables, a steeply pitched roof and a three-story turret. I especially liked playing in the round rooms of the tower; I felt like I was in a castle.

This house was central to my grandmother's life. On October 4, 1910, she married my grandfather in the first floor sitting room, inside the bay window. Throughout their lives, my grandparents lived in various places in Warren, Pennsylvania and Canada, but when the Honorable Frank M. Knapp died in 1928, my grandparents moved into the big house to care for my great-grandmother until her death in November, 1936. It was a wonderful, old house with a grand, curved staircase leading to a wide, second floor hallway. Three bedrooms, a living room and dining room, all with oriental carpets accenting the hardwood floors, three bathrooms with marble tubs and sinks and brass fixtures and a linen room opened onto this hallway. The kitchen was situated off the dining room. The first and

**GREAT-GRANDMOTHER
ROSAMOND ENSWORTH KNAPP**

GRANDPARENTS HOME ON SECOND AVENUE

third floors had more bedrooms and seating areas, which my grandparents ultimately turned into apartments and rented. A Swedish woman who spoke little English took care of the house, did the ironing and such. She didn't talk much, but even when she did, I couldn't understand her.

Grandma and Grandpa had a big wall cabinet at the end of the stairs where they kept all the toys and games: puzzles, the Pollyanna board game, balls and jacks, dominos, coloring books and crayons, checkers. I always lost myself in there for a few hours. If Aunt Roanie was on leave from the service—she was a Wave stationed in New York—she kept me occupied. She taught me to ride the small, two-wheeled bicycle stored in the basement of the big house. She showed me how to dive off the platform at Lake Chautauqua. She took me on my first terrifying ride on a wooden roller coaster at the Celeron, New York amusement park, just across the Pennsylvania state line. I screamed through the entire ride while Aunt Roanie countered with her loud, boisterous laugh. With a strong desire for adventure and a good sense of humor, Aunt Roanie was great fun to be with.

MY GRANDFATHER, Clifton Pratt DeLong, worked in the property tax division at the Warren County Courthouse. His dad, Herman R. DeLong, married

JEAN, KAYE, AUNT ROANIE AND DONNIE TAKING A DIP – 1940

a woman named Mayme Pratt, and worked as a butcher until his death on April 17, 1917 of unknown causes. Mayme remarried a man named Black a year later.

If questioned about his family tree, Grandpa always laughed and said, "I come from a line of Clarion County horse thieves." Maybe that's where I got my love of horses, even though I never stole one. Grandpa was rotund and stood only 5' 5" tall. His wire-rimmed glasses accented his especially round face.

Lucile Knapp DeLong was my grandmother's name, and she looked like the typical grandmother—only 5' 2" tall, buxom with a curve-less figure, no hips, resulting from the stiff corset she always wore, sharp features, softened by the short, permed hair outlining her face.

Grandma DeLong was brought up in a refined household. She carried her genteel approach to life into her marriage and allowed others to take care of the house while she involved herself in more important activities—being a good wife and mother and a gifted soprano. She took singing lessons to improve her voice and sang in the Presbyterian Church choir. But Grandma DeLong loved to cook and arrange Sunday dinners, and going to Grandma and Grandpa's house for dinner was a special event.

We always put on our party manners and dressed in our Sunday best. Mom painstakingly brushed my long hair, tying it up with ribbons, sometimes braiding it. Grandma Delong

DAD AND HIS FATHER - 1915

felt sorry for Mom that she had to deal with my unruly locks, so she paid for me to go to the beauty shop every week to have my hair washed and dried.

I got to wear my black, patent leather shoes I made shine by polishing them with Vaseline. I adored those shoes. We didn't have a vehicle, so my grandparents came to pick us up in their big, fancy car. I loved walking up the slate sidewalk to my grandparents' home, listening to the click

JEAN'S LONG HAIR

of the hard leather heels on the pavement and seeing my reflection in the shiny leather. It's a wonder I didn't run into something and break my neck.

As soon as we walked into the big house, the most delicious aromas came wafting down the stairs, enticing us up to the second floor. We climbed the stairs and took seats in the living room to discuss the week's events and news with my grandparents. Our baby sister Linda slept in a bassinet next to my parents, not knowing anything about all the interesting places in this house. I decided to show her later, when she got bigger. Before long, Grandma and Grandpa went back into the kitchen to put the finishing touches on dinner.

Donnie and Kaye worked quietly on a puzzle off in the corner of the room. I sat in one of the Victorian chairs, still staring at my feet, admiring my shoes. My feet just dangled in mid-air while all the grownups' feet were securely planted on the nice oriental rugs. I scooted forward to the edge of the chair and stretched my legs as far as they would go, trying to touch the floor, but it didn't help. After deciding I couldn't solve this problem without growing, I turned my attention elsewhere.

First, I picked up the Sunday newspaper, plopped down on the floor and read the funnies. I loved the smell of ink and enjoyed leafing through the pages, picking out the words I understood. I felt so grown up reading the newspaper. I grew bored with this after a while and wended my way down the hallway, through the dining room with the long, dark table and carved chairs and into the kitchen, the source of all those tantalizing smells swirling around the house. There I found Grandma and Grandpa, working side-

THE DELONG CLAN – 1943

by-side. While Grandma dished up the mashed potatoes and gravy and fresh peas and carrots, Grandpa carved the large, beef roast. They worked together quietly but efficiently, and soon everyone was seated at the table, which was dressed in Grandma's best linens, china and crystal. She even had little crystal salt containers that we dipped our celery and carrots into. Grandpa said a quick blessing, and we started passing around dishes, piled high with delicious food.

Sunday dinner was a time for the grownups to talk. Donnie, Kaye and I didn't speak unless directly addressed. We watched our manners and did as Mom and Dad had taught us. *Mabel, Mabel, if you're able, get your elbows off the table* was one of their favorite sayings.

Sometimes in the afternoons following lunch, Grandpa took us for rides around Warren in his big, black car before bringing us home.

THESE DINNERS and the time spent in my grandparents' home hold wonderful memories for me. Even though the house was beautiful and decorated with refined and expensive furnishings, it was a well lived-in house. My curiosity was welcomed, so I explored, examined, and touched anything I wanted to.

I wish I had spent more time with my grandparents and gotten to know them better. My grandfather left an envelope bearing my name, which contained important papers and the family tree on my grandmother's side, when he died in St. Petersburg, Florida on June 17, 1963. After his death, my grandmother moved back to Warren, Pennsylvania and lived with my Aunt Roanie and her husband, Bill Lawhead, until her death on December 18, 1970.

KAYE, DONNIE AND JEAN
AT THE WARREN RESERVOIR - 1940

FAMILY PHOTOGRAPH

Mom Loved Me Best

IALWAYS KNEW MOM loved me best. I never questioned my standing in her heart until I was sent to the Andersons' house in North Warren where my parents' good friend, Millie, lived. I was seven years old and too young to stay at home while my mother gave birth to my sister Linda at the hospital. Donnie and Kaye were older and could stay alone while Daddy worked. Mom tried to convince me of the good time I'd have by reminding me of the picnics we enjoyed at the Andersons' house, the animals there and the barn, so off I went, reluctantly.

The Andersons lived three miles from our house in a white, clapboard farmhouse in North Warren built into the side of a steep hill. When people walked through the front door from the street, they were on the second floor. I found it interesting that half of the house was below street level. The upper floor had a small, cozy living room, three bedrooms and a bath. A dining room with a pine table and chairs, a pantry and a huge, country kitchen made up the ground floor, and it was all presided over by Millie's mother, Agnes Anderson.

Even with the cows, dogs and fish, I didn't have much to do at the Andersons' house. Sometimes I sat in the dining room and watched Mrs. Anderson cook, can and make pies. She was a buxom, stocky woman with a long, gray braid hanging down her back. The stern look on her face kept me at a safe distance as she moved around the kitchen in a determined way. Her heavy hands carried large buckets of water and feed to the animals out back with little or no problem.

Mostly I stayed outside and played with the wirehaired fox terriers and

JEAN IN THE ANDERSONS'
FISH POND

Boston terriers the Andersons raised and sold. The Andersons kept the dogs tied to their doghouses and didn't play with them much, so they weren't very well mannered. They jumped all over me, almost knocking me down, licked me in the face and scratched me with their long claws. They meant no harm; they were just starved for attention. I also explored the big white barn filled with hay or roamed the pasture and garden, which bordered on Conewango *Crick* down a bit from the Wetmore Eddy. But my favorite place was the small, cement pond filled with the biggest, most colorful goldfish I had ever seen; these white and orange fish must have been at least ten or twelve inches long. The heat was terrible that August, and many times, I took off my sunsuit and waded into the fishpond with the koi to cool off. They didn't seem to mind. Without the dogs and the fish, I would have been totally miserable at the Andersons' house.

One day, Millie's father, Mr. Anderson, took me down to the field to check the garden and bring back some ripe tomatoes and green beans to fix for dinner. Mr. Anderson was a tall, thin man who had very little to say. His weathered face, large rough hands and slightly stooped shoulders came from the many years of hard work required on a farm. He had a large garden where he grew lettuce, peas, corn, potatoes and many other vegetables as well as the tomatoes and green beans we went to get that day. I had to go to the bathroom when we started out, but I was too bashful to say anything. I just prayed that I could hold it long enough to get back to the house. As we walked along the *crick*, heading back to the house, I felt a warm rush running down my pant legs and into my shoes. Mortified, I just stood there paralyzed. Mr. Anderson stopped, turned around and gazed down at me, "Did you wet your pants?"

"No sir," I lied. "I fell into the *crick* and got wet."

"I know you didn't fall in, Jean."

"Yes, I did. Really, I did," I sobbed. "I want to go home to my house, where I live."

Mr. Anderson began walking again, and I followed him. "Now, go ask Mrs. Anderson to change your clothes."

I stood in front of Mrs. Anderson and told her I fell in the

MOM AND LITTLE SISTER LINDA, VISITING THE NEIGHBORS

crick, I needed clean clothes, and I wanted to go home. She leaned over and stared at me, then said, "You know, Jean, your mom has a new baby now. She doesn't love you anymore."

I MADE IT THROUGH the next couple of days, and finally, Millie took me home. Before the car even stopped, I jumped out, sped up the front steps, swung the door open, and ran into the house. "Where's Mom," I shouted to my sister Kaye.

"She's upstairs in bed. She just got back from the hospital today."

I flew up the stairs into her bedroom and wrapped my arms around Mom and would not let go. Eventually she eased me back and asked if I wanted to see my new sister. I agreed because it seemed important to her. I glanced down in the bassinet and saw a pretty baby girl with just a wisp of brown hair, sleeping and then went back and sat at my mother's side. I stayed there most of the next week, making sure I wasn't being replaced by this new arrival.

As my sister Linda grew up, I didn't have much to do with her. I saw her as a rival for my parents' attention, and she just didn't like to do the same things I did. She preferred sitting quietly, playing with her dolls, rather than being outside, looking for adventure. For years, I did not tell my mother what Mrs. Anderson said to me that day. Until I did, my mother never understood why I ignored Linda. It wasn't until we were adults that Linda and I forged a strong relationship.

Janet

J ANET CARLSON lived across the road from me on Kenmore Street. We were the same age, but that was where our similarities ended. We looked different. A tall, thin girl with blond hair, blue eyes and fair skin, Janet was always taken for someone from Sweden. I was short, had long, brown hair and dark skin, especially in the summertime.

Our temperaments differed significantly as well. Even though I was quick tempered and strong willed, I always stood up for the underdog, and at times, I could be very gullible. Janet often took advantage of me. Many times I went home mad because of something Janet did or said. I especially hated it when she cheated at games. When we played jacks, she moved the pieces, then denied it and continued to play.

Janet looked for ways to get to me. She pulled my hair braids. She hid my skate key, so I couldn't tighten my roller skates. One time we came across a big, black snake that looked fearsome, so we started throwing rocks at it. I then felt sorry for the snake and tried to get Janet to stop flinging rocks at it. She wouldn't, so I pushed her every time she got ready to toss a rock, throwing off her aim. She never quit tormenting the poor snake. Finally she pushed me to the ground, and we both went home mad.

Janet also had a mean-natured sense humor. While we played one Saturday, Janet asked, "Hey Jean, you want to go to church with me tomorrow morning?"

I knew she went to Calvary Baptist Church. I didn't know much about the Baptists. I went to Sunday school at the First Presbyterian Church, and

I didn't like it very much. One of my first times there, the teacher reprimanded me for talking in class, so I disliked everything about the place. I asked Janet, "Maybe, I'll go. What do they do at your church?"

"Well, you go inside the front door, and someone meets you there," Janet said. "They walk you down this long hall into a big room, and there, you take off your socks and shoes."

I thought that was mighty strange, but I said, "Okay, I can do that."

Janet continued, "Then you take off your dress and slip and go to church in your underpants."

I saw myself, standing there in nothing but my best underwear. "No way is anybody going to make me undress," I spit back to her. "I'm not ever going to your church."

Janet laughed and laughed. "You're so dumb," she said. "You'll believe anything." Then she laughed some more. I stomped off and went back home, swearing to myself that I'd never play with Janet again.

My resolve to stay away from Janet never lasted. After a few days passed, I'd forget about our fight and go back over to her house to play. Janet had the ability to be a lot of fun, if she chose to. Plus she lived right across the street, so she was a convenient playmate.

I didn't know what it meant at the time, but the grownups said Janet's dad, Mr. Carlson, was an alcoholic, but he *got religion*. All I knew was that the refrigerator in Mr. Carlson's auto-body shop was full of bottles of Coca-Cola and nothing else. When he wasn't there, Janet and I drank cokes and spun around in his office chair until we got sick.

Sometimes Mom allowed me to sleep over at Janet's house. Her father repaired school buses, so Janet and I took blankets and pillows and slept on the seats in the bus. We brought along cookies and crackers and soda pop, so we didn't get hungry or thirsty. What we didn't anticipate was the need to go to the bathroom. The bus didn't have a toilet, and both of us were too afraid to go outside in the middle of the night. With practice, we learned how to pee in the pop bottles after we drank the soda. It took determination, but we persevered until we were accomplished bottle *pee-ers*. In the mornings, we emptied our bottles in the grass.

JANET'S MOTHER had a stocky frame with large breasts. At times, Janet and I hung out in the kitchen while her mom prepared a meal, and we begged her to sing us a sad song. "Please, please, please, sing us a sad song," we chanted. I loved sad songs. She hemmed and hawed for a good fifteen minutes before finally relenting. I always thought she just liked the sound of us begging.

She didn't even need to warm up her beautiful soprano voice. She immediately launched into the first verse of "Come Home Father" with its haunting lyrics.

Come Home Father

'Tis the
song of little Mary,
Standing at the bar-room door
While the shameful midnight revel
Rages wildly as before.

Father, dear father, come home with me, now!
The clock on the steeple strikes one;
You said you were coming straight home from the shop,
As soon as your day's work was done.
Our fire has gone out our house is all dark,
And mother's been waiting since tea,
With poor brother Benny so sick in her arms,
And no one to help her but me.
Come home, come home, come home!
Please father, dear father come home.

Hear the sweet voice of the child,
Which the night winds repeat as they roam!
Oh who could resist this most plaintive of cries,
Please father dear father come home.

Father, dear father, come home with me, now!
The clock on the steeple strikes two;
The night has grown colder and Benny is worse,
But he has been calling for you.
Indeed he is worse, Ma says he will die
Perhaps before morning shall dawn;
And this is the message she sent me to bring,
"Come quickly! Or he will be gone."
Come home, come home, come home!
Please father, dear father come home

Hear the sweet voice of the child,
Which the night winds repeat as they roam!

Oh who could resist this most plaintive of cries,
Please father dear father come home.

Father, dear father, come home with me, now!
The clock on the steeple strikes three,
The house is so lonely, the hours are so long
For poor weeping mother and me.
Yes we are alone. Poor Benny is dead
And gone with the angels of light,
And these were the very last words that he said
"I want to kiss Papa goodnight."
Come home, come home, come home!
Please father, dear father come home.

Hear the sweet voice of the child,
Which the night winds repeat as they roam!
Oh who could resist this most plaintive of cries,
Please father dear father come home.

(Lyrics based on the poem of Henry Clay Work – 1864)

JANET AND I SAT AT HER FEEt and cried and cried. I pictured the whole scene—poor, little Mary standing at the barroom door pleading with her father, her momma holding her sick brother, the wind howling—everything played like a picture show in my mind. We pleaded for another song, but she only sang that one, never more and never a different song. Maybe that was the only tune she knew. Eventually, we got tired of begging and went back outside to play.

Janet came to my house sometimes, and we matched wits in the alphabet game. "A – my name is Alice. My husband's name is Andy; we come from Alabama, and we sell apples. B – my name is Betty, and my husband's name is Bob. We used to live in Boston, and we sell beans." The game went on like that until one of us messed up. Then it was the other's turn. Some days we played hopscotch. More often than not, we got into a fight, and one of us went home mad.

IF IT WAS AN ESPECIALLY boring day, Janet went across the street to her house and got her red wagon with the detachable, wooden sides. We pulled the wagon behind us as we went to the vacant lot next door to Mrs. Hayes' house. Snakes, lots of them, sunned themselves here. They were all logy and warm in the afternoon sun, so we crept up and grabbed them by their tails.

We filled the wagon with fifteen to twenty snakes and threw in a couple of toads, just to see what the snakes would do. Nothing ever happened, so we dumped them on the sidewalk, so we could catch them again on the next boring day.

ONE FRIDAY MORNING in 1945 when I was ten years old, Janet called and asked if I wanted to go to Canada with her and her family. They had a cabin there, and every summer, they spent two weeks in Canada when Mr. Carlson took his vacation. Janet said they were leaving the next morning. The hot, humid days of summer stretched on in Warren, and the cool weather of Canada sounded like a wonderful idea to me.

I hung up the receiver and hurried into the kitchen where Mom was cleaning up the breakfast dishes. "Mom, Janet's on the phone and is asking me if I want to go to Canada for two weeks with them." Before she could say anything, I pleaded, "Please, please, can I go?"

"You know, Jean, all you and Janet do is fight. Are you sure you want to spend two weeks with her?" Mom asked.

"Yes, yes, it will be fun. I promise to be on my best behavior. Mom, please?"

"Okay, Jean, you can go if you behave yourself."

I picked up the phone and gave the operator Janet's number. "Janet, I can go. I'll see you tomorrow at 6:00. I got to go pack some warm clothes."

I WAS SO EXCITED I didn't sleep at all that night. We left at 6:00 a.m. the next day. Going to Canada was thrilling, but driving there in a car was more good news than I could stand. Our family didn't have a car, so we either walked or rode the bus everywhere. When my parents had an extra-large load of groceries, they took a taxi home. I thought about the things I'd see out of the car window on our way to Canada. *Maybe even some horses.* Mr. and Mrs. Carlson sat comfortably in the front seat, but the backseat was crowded with Janet, her older sister Lois and me. Luckily, I sat next to the door and could see everything out the window.

Lois was only a few years older than Janet and I, but she treated us like babies who didn't know *anything.* She developed early and had breasts, which made her think she was better than us. She was a pretty girl with shoulder length light brown hair and blue eyes who turned a few heads especially when she strutted around in front of every good looking guy.

Our destination was North Bay in Northeastern Ontario. We spent the eight hours in the car playing tic-tac-toe, looking for Pennsylvania license plates, cars of the same color and any other game we could think up. I won hands down in the I Spy Horses and Cows game.

When we reached the Canadian border, we stopped to visit Niagara Falls. The roar of the water crashing at the bottom of the falls was deafening. I felt its power in my chest, and the sensation paralyzed me. This was my second visit, and still, I could not force myself to walk up to the fence for a better look. I didn't have to go to the edge to see the boiling, frothy rush of water pouring over the falls; I was close enough. As glad as I was to see such an amazing sight again, I was relieved when everyone got their fill, and we left.

Mr. Carlson showed his driver's license to the official at the end of the bridge, and we crossed into Canada. With approximately five hours driving time left to reach the cabin at North Bay, we continued on for a couple of hours, stopped briefly for a picnic lunch at a roadside park and got back on the road.

"Look, kids, up ahead is the Dionne quintuplet's house," said Mr. Carlson, pointing out an old wooden house with posts holding up the roof. The five identical sisters were born in 1934, only a year before me, near the village of Corbeil and became the first quintuplets to survive infancy. They lived in this tiny farmhouse with their five older brothers and sisters. We strained our eyes, hoping to see anything that looked like a quint, but no one was around.

A short time later, we turned off the main highway and made our way down a one-way, dirt road deep into the woods. "Look, Janet, at those beautiful trees with the white bark," I said. Mr. Carlson informed us that they were birch trees, and the Indians used them to make canoes many years ago. "Can we get out and look at one?" I asked.

"No, not now," he said, "we're almost to the cabin. There are lots of them there that you can examine."

I was so antsy and ready to get out of the car. I had sat still for eight hours; that was a record for me. Before Mr. Carlson came to a complete stop at the cabin, I jumped out of the car and looked all around. This was the most beautiful, magical place I had ever seen. Huge fir trees that smelled like Christmas surrounded the cabin, and pine needles covered the ground like a soft carpet. I walked over to a white-barked birch tree and ran my hand over its soft, smooth bark. The bark came off easily, like the skin of an onion; it was thin and felt like velvet. The tree's scent was unlike anything I had ever smelled, deep and woodsy. I collected a few more pieces of bark to keep with me and smell any time I wanted.

The log cabin was rustic but had all the modern conveniences of home, even an indoor toilet. The place smelled a little musty because it had been closed up all winter and spring. To take the chill out of the fifty-degree evening air, Mr. Carlson brought in logs for the fireplace and built a roaring fire while we unpacked. Mrs. Carlson fixed a small meal for dinner, and Janet and I climbed between clean sheets and soft blankets and drifted off to sleep, thinking about all the adventures to come in this beautiful Canadian forest.

JANET IN CANADA THE FOLLOWING YEAR

I AWOKE TO THE SMELL of bacon, eggs and pancakes Mrs. Carlson prepared and placed on the kitchen table with cocoa and coffee for everyone to enjoy. Janet and I gobbled our breakfast and ran out the door to investigate our surroundings. We headed to the blue lake. Off in the misty distance was a lone cabin perched on a rocky shoreline with no signs of life. It felt strange knowing we were the only people on the lake at this time of year, but we did have a telephone and a radio, so we weren't completely isolated.

Janet and I explored the edge of the lake, looking for shells and flat stones to skip across the water and wading in the shallows. The water was clear and as cold as ice, too cold for swimming. We spent the day investigating everything within shouting distance of Janet's parents. They didn't want us to go too far away because there were bears and moose close by. I thought it would be great to see a wild animal, but the Carlsons preferred that we not run into one. Lois was far too grown up to join Janet and me on our adventures. She preferred to stay in the cabin and help her mother. How boring!

ONE DAY, MR. CARLSON decided to take out the motor boat he kept at the empty cabin across the lake. After he retrieved the boat from the shed, we loaded up the fishing gear and off we went. The cool air whistled in my ears as we tore across the lake and rounded a point to an even greater stretch of water. It seemed endless. Finally we stopped; Mr. Carlson threw in his line, and we sat and listened to the stillness. The only sound to break the silence was the occasional sad cry of a loon or the honking of geese off in the distance.

Janet and I didn't fish on this trip, so I had plenty of time for my imagination to run wild. It was just the three of us on this huge lake—we never saw another person our entire time at the cabin. What if something happened? There was no one around to rescue us. The water beneath us was cold and deep, and I *knew* sea serpents had to be down there, waiting to get us. When Mr. Carlson yelled, I almost jumped out of the boat.

"Oh, my. What do we have here?" Mr. Carlson cried. "There's something on my line, and it's heading out to the middle of the lake." He grabbed the pole and jerked it to set the hook. I knew it was a good size fish because it bent his pole in half. Mr. Carlson kept the line taut and let the fish tire himself out before he slowly reeled in the beast. He used the net to lift the fish into the boat. "Look what we have here," he said with a big smile, "a Northern pike. Good-sized one, too. It must be at least fifteen or sixteen pounds. Looks like we're having fish for dinner tonight."

I had never seen a pike before, and it looked scary. I gave it a lot of room as it flopped around the bottom of the boat. It was about thirty-six inches long with a gray body, a long, rounded snout and a mouth full of needle-sharp teeth. I didn't put my hands anywhere near his mouth. Mr. Carlson picked him up and threw him in the fish box, and then we headed back to the cabin to get the pike ready for dinner. The sun was just beginning to set, making the lake look red with sparkling beads of clear water from the boat skimming across its surface. *Red sky at night, sailor's delight.* This night was truly a delight. It had been a perfect day, now a perfect night. This was almost heaven; the only thing missing was my gallant steed. Surely, he was waiting for me in my dreams.

THE DAYS AT THE CABIN in Canada flew by, and I lost track of how many times Janet and I argued. Thankfully, the fights were short lived because something always caught our attention, and then we'd be off on an adventure somewhere, forgetting about our disagreement.

ON AUGUST 14, 1945, we walked into the cabin to the screams and shouts of Mrs. Carlson, "The war is over; the war is over. Hallelujah! We just heard it on the radio. I think we should have a prayer and thank the Lord." We all joined hands and prayed. Afterward, she and Lois went off to the kitchen to make popcorn and fudge to celebrate this great day.

I knew little about the war. My uncles were soldiers, but I wasn't sure what they did. Mom used ration stamps to buy sugar, butter, cheese and other foods, and I understood that was because of the war. With so many men drafted into active duty, Dad had to help out at the post office in Indiantown Gap, some two hundred miles from home. He was gone at least a month or two. I didn't know much about Hitler, the Nazis or the two atomic bombs dropped on Japan, but based on Mrs. Carlson's excitement, I recognized that this was an important day.

Janet and I thought this occasion deserved a song, so we asked Mrs. Carlson to sing us a new, sad ballad. Because she was so happy that the war was over, she relented. As she stirred the fudge, she sang the following:

In the Baggage Coach Ahead

On a dark stormy night as the train rattled on,
All the passengers had gone to bed,
Except one young man with a babe in his arms
Who sat there with a bowed head.
The innocent one began crying just then,
As though its poor heart would break.
One angry man said, "Make that child stop its noise,
For its keeping all of us awake."

"Put it out," said another, "Don't keep it in here;
We've paid for our berths and want rest."
But never a word said the man with the child,
As he fondled it close to his breast.
"Where is its mother? Go take it to her,"
This a lady then softly said.
"I wish that I could" was the man's sad reply,
"But she's dead in the coach ahead."

While the train rolled onward, a husband sat in tears,
Thinking of the happiness of just a few short years.
Baby's face brings pictures of a cherished hope that's dead,
But baby's cries can't waken her in the baggage coach ahead

Every eye filled with tears when his story he told
Of a wife who was faithful and true,
He told how he'd saved all his earnings for years,
Just to build up a home for two,
How, when Heaven had sent them this sweet little babe,
Their young happy lives were blessed;
His heart seemed to break when he mentioned her name,
And in tears tried to tell them the rest,

Every woman arose to assist with the child,
There were mothers and wives on that train,
And soon was the little one sleeping in peace,
With no tho't of sorrow or pain.
Next morn at a station he bade all goodbye,
"God bless you," he softly said,
Each one had a story to tell in their home,
Of the baggage coach ahead.

GUSSIE DAVIS
1896

JANET AND I STOOD in the kitchen, tears running down our cheeks. We thanked Mrs. Carlson for the beautiful song and went into the living room to wait for the popcorn and fudge. Not long after the treats, Janet and I went to bed. It had been a tiring day. In the darkness, we planned our adventures for the next day for soon we would be leaving this paradise in the woods.

Suddenly, we heard a loud, deep bellowing not far from our cabin. I bolted upright and asked, "What in the world is that?"

"Just a moose," Janet said. "Go back to sleep."

ALL JANET AND I DID on our last day in the woods was fight. We had spent more time together than we ever had, plus I was homesick and missed my family. Lois and Mrs. Carlson cleaned up the cabin while Mr. Carlson took the boat back to the neighbors across the lake for storage. Janet and I cleaned up outside and argued all day long.

The eight-hour ride home was quiet. We were all exhausted and ready to get back to our normal lives. When the Carlsons dropped me off at home, my family was glad to see me, even my brother and sisters. My two weeks in North Bay, Canada were amazing, but now I was home and ready to get back to school. In just a few weeks, I'd be starting the fifth grade at Home Street School. One adventure was ending and a new one beginning.

Men in White Coats

I STARED AT THE BLACKBOARD from the back of the classroom, trying to make out what my third grade teacher, Miss Erikson, wrote on the board. If I closed my eyes just right, I could just make out the letters and numbers. Miss Erikson caught me squinting and asked, "Jean, can you see the blackboard?"

"No ma'am. It's blurry," I said.

"Then come up here and trade seats with Donald Adams." I got my books and papers together and moved up to a desk in the front row. "Is that better, Jean?"

"Yes ma'am, a lot better." Everything on the board was still blurry, but at least, I could make out the marks. Miss Erikson sent a note home to my parents, advising that I get an eye exam as soon as possible. Mom immediately made an appointment with Dr. Helmbrecht.

Dr. Helmbrecht was a kindly man, tall and thin with sharp features and a great deal of patience. He turned the lights out and showed a bunch of letters on the far wall. I could see the big "E" at the top and a couple of the ones under it that were going in all different directions, but other than that, everything was one big blur. He gave me a piece of cardboard and had me use it to cover one eye and then the other and asked me to call out the numbers and letters I could make out. Then he had me look through this black, mask-looking thing he kept changing and asked me which one made me see better. When he finished, he said, "Well, young lady, you are quite nearsighted. You are going to need glasses."

I looked through the frames covering one whole wall and picked out a pair of round, wire-rimmed glasses, not concerned about how they looked on me. A week later, my glasses were ready. I could not believe what I saw the first time I put them on; a whole new world opened up to me. I stared at everything—clouds, birds, butterflies, trees, flowers, everything—not able to get enough of looking at each little thing in a brand new light. It was almost too much to bear. All my girlfriends tried on my new glasses and couldn't see a thing, but now I saw it all.

THAT SAME YEAR I also had a lot of earaches, which sent me to the couch in the living room with a warm washcloth against my ear to ease the pain. Some days, I couldn't even go to school, but Miss Erikson dropped my homework off every day, so I wouldn't fall behind.

Dr. Larson made house calls and came by to see me one day. He felt my neck, looked in my ears and then down my throat. "Mrs. DeLong, your daughter has bad tonsils, and they have to come out," he told my mother. I didn't know what that meant or how Dr. Larson was going to get my tonsils out, but I was scared and refused to discuss the whole situation. My earache eventually got better, and I put Dr. Larson and my tonsils out of my mind, until the next time I ran a temperature and had to miss more school.

ONE DAY MOM TOLD ME she had an errand to run, and we were going for a little ride with Millie, so I climbed into the backseat and peered out of the window with my new eyes that could see everything. I was always excited to be going someplace new. After twenty minutes and a thousand questions about where we were going, Mom pulled into the WCA (Woman's Christian Association) Hospital in Jamestown, New York.

Mom grabbed me by the hand and walked me up the steps while I asked over and over again, "What are we doing here?"

"Jean, I have to drop off something," she said. We walked into an office where a woman directed us down the hall to a little room with a small bed in it.

"Mom, why are we here?" I asked again. This time more sternly.

"You're here to have your tonsils out, Jean, so you'll feel better." As she gave me the dreadful news, several people, including two men, in nurses' uniforms came into the room and tried to coax me into taking off my clothes. No way was that going to happen.

"No, no, no," I screamed as I turned to run from the room, but the army of white coats blocked the door.

I STRUGGLED TO GET AWAY, but the biggest one of the bunch grabbed me by the waist and lifted me off the floor while one took off my shoes, another slipped off my pants, a third pulled my shirt over my head and the last one smiled at me in a kind way and wrapped me in a hospital gown. As soon as the big one let me go, I flung myself into my mother's arms and locked my arms around her neck.

"Now, Jean," Mother said in a calm, quiet voice, "you know how many earaches and sore throats you've had, how much time you were sick on the couch and couldn't go out and play." I couldn't argue with that. "We have to do something about your tonsils. You'll feel so much better once your tonsils are gone." Mom carried me over to the little white bed, laid me down and pulled a scratchy sheet up to my neck. She moved a chair next to the bed and sat close to me, stroking my hair. "Someone is going to come in soon and give you a little pill that is going to make you feel better. Okay, honey?" I nodded, all the fight had gone out of me.

I lay there shaking, feeling like a trapped animal. I was drowning in white; everything in this room was white, and with each breath, the alcohol-steeped air sickened my stomach. I listened for footsteps, my senses on high alert for danger, but for a time, all I heard were murmurs of conversations in the distance and the squeaky wheels of gurneys being pushed up and down the hallway. I jumped when the nurse opened the door and walked in with a glass of water and a tiny white pill. She handed both to my mother and left the room. "Here, Jean," Mom said, "take this and when you wake up, you'll feel a whole lot better. You'll have all the vanilla ice cream you can eat, and then we'll go home. I promise." I took a gulp of the water and swallowed the pill. I drifted off to sleep not knowing who or what to believe anymore.

I WOKE UP IN A STRANGE BED with my throat burning like a bonfire and Mom sitting beside me. "Hi Jean, do you want a sip of water or maybe some ice cream?" she asked. Big tears ran down my cheeks, but I stopped crying because my throat hurt too much. I settled for the ice cream, but it was plain, old vanilla and didn't taste good. Lying in that little bed, I felt scared, miserable and dejected until I finally fell back asleep.

The next morning, Mom and Millie brought me home and put me in my own bed to recuperate. I spent the next few days between my bed and the couch, and slowly began to feel well enough to eat solid food. Mom fixed me macaroni and cheese, my favorite, and I gulped down the entire plate. After not eating for three or four days, I was starving. I went back and sat on the couch and started to feel sick to my stomach. A moment later, I upchucked the macaroni and cheese, but now it looked more like pasta and tomato sauce.

Mom scooped me up and rushed me to Dr. Larson's office. He looked down my throat and said my stitches had broken. We raced back to the hospital. This time I went willingly because I thought I was bleeding to death. Everything related to the second surgery was a blur. I survived, but the experience instilled in me a fear of hospitals and men in white coats that exists to this day.

STICKY, GOOEY CANDY like Sugar Daddies and the chocolate-covered Sugar Mamas tasted great, but they pulled out my fillings, which meant a trip to see Dr. Sedgewick, our dentist. Dr. Sedgewick terrified me. Because I was just as scared of needles as I was of the dentist, Dr. Sedgewick never gave me novocaine to numb the pain when he replaced my fillings. I squirmed and groaned in pain the whole time he drilled. Then the drill heated up and hurt even more. When I finally got out of his chair, I swore I'd never eat Sugar Daddies again, but that never lasted.

My brother Donnie was smart and insisted on novocaine, before he let Dr. Sedgewick drill. One day, Donnie came back from a visit to the dentist with a big ball of mercury in a swish cup. He poured the mercury onto the dining room table, and we played with it for hours, separating the ball and watching it meld together when we rolled the sections toward each other. Then we shined up some silver dimes with the mercury. We rolled it around and around until it finally dropped on the floor and exploded into a thousand pieces we couldn't put back together. I always wondered where that mercury went.

Norma

MY FRIEND NORMA ELLBERG lived on Connecticut Avenue, about a block and a half away, in a house with a huge basement with a smooth, painted concrete floor perfect for roller skating. On our walks home from school, I regularly stopped off to get my skates and key and met Norma a few minutes later at her house. The Ellbergs' basement had very little in it—a couple of chairs, a Victrola record player and a furnace in the far corner that we zipped around with lightning speed on the smooth concrete floor. Norma's curly brown hair bounced as she skated, and her blue eyes shone brighter than ever when she was happy.

We played our favorite cowboy tunes on the Victrola, turning up the volume as loud as the phonograph allowed. Then we circled the basement to the sounds of Gene Autry as he sang "Back in the Saddle Again" and Roy Rogers and Dale Evans, wishing us "...happy trails...until we meet again." We crooned with the greats and longed for a "...home where the buffalo roam, where the deer and antelope play, where seldom is heard a discouraging word, and the sky is not cloudy all day."

Sometimes we went so fast that we fell and skinned our knees, but we didn't care. We just got up and kept going until we were exhausted, or it was time for dinner.

NORMA'S OLDER SISTER, Jean, was supposed to be watching us because both Mr. and Mrs. Ellberg worked, but we rarely saw her. She never came out of her bedroom, which was just as well. Jean was a beautiful girl, but she never smiled. She looked like a model, every hair in place, but she was so dull, no personality at all, just like her father. Watching an apple turn brown was more exciting than talking with Mr. Ellberg or Jean. If I could get Jean to say two words, it was a big deal. Thankfully, Norma took after her mother.

Mrs. Ellberg was colorful in every way. She dyed her short, bobbed hair pitch black, painted her lips and nails blood red and wore brightly colored dresses and worked in an office, which was unusual in those days. Her sense of style extended to their house as well with the walls in several rooms painted lavender and the kitchen bright yellow. I marveled at all the colors and sat on the edge of a living room chair—not wanting to wrinkle the fabric—and took in the many shades surrounding me. This room was one to be looked at, not lived in. While I liked all the colors, I didn't stay in the living room very long; no one ever spent any time there. The lamps or knick-knacks were touched only to be dusted. It was a showcase of Mrs. Ellberg's talent.

Norma's house always smelled like stale tobacco as both her parents were chain smokers and left many butts in ashtrays throughout the house. Sometimes when no one was there besides us and Norma's invisible sister, we pulled out the longest butts, straightened them out and lit them with kitchen matches. Then we sat at the table just like her parents did and sucked on those cigarettes. It all seemed very adult until the coughing started when we tried to inhale.

EVERY TIME I LEFT Norma's house, I saw Nancy Smail, walking around in her parents' backyard next door. A chain-link fence surrounded the neighbor's yard, so Nancy could go outside without her parents worrying that she'd wander off. A few years older than me, Nancy was very sweet, but I knew something was wrong with her. She wasn't quite right in the head and had slanted eyes—I later learned that she had Downs Syndrome—but I stood at the fence and tried to talk with her before going home. She only said a few, one-syllable words and didn't pay attention for long, so it was always a short conversation.

ONE SUNDAY, the telephone rang, and it was Norma, "Hey Jeannie, Mom and Dad and I are going to my grandma's house. Do you want to come?"

"Where does she live?" I asked.

"Oh, she lives in North Warren on Jackson Run Road, out in the country."

Hearing the word *country* always interested me because of the critters I might find there—butterflies, toads, snakes, rabbits. I didn't really want to meet her grandmother; she was probably as humorless as Norma's father.

I put my hand over the receiver, "Mom, can I go with Norma to her grandma's house today? She lives in North Warren."

"Okay, Jean. Please behave yourself," Mom answered.

"Norma, Mom says I can go. What time are you picking me up?"

"We'll leave around one o'clock, after Grandma comes home from church."

RIGHT ON TIME, Norma and her parents pulled up in front of my house and honked the horn. I climbed into the back seat next to Norma, and we began the twenty-minute trip. Thankfully, her boring sister stayed home; she would have ruined the adventure for everyone. Grandma's house was an old, rickety, one-story farmhouse in need of a good paint job, and it didn't have any indoor plumbing. After I met Grandma, Norma and I headed out the door to see what we could find.

First we had to examine the outhouse because I had never seen one before. I expected to find Sears Roebuck catalogs, but Grandma only had cheap toilet paper. The smell surrounding the outhouse wasn't pleasant, but the many mothballs scattered around it made the stench somewhat better.

With our curiosity satisfied, we went off into the field in search of something interesting. Right away we found a huge toad, scrunched down in the tall grass, hoping we wouldn't see him. I picked him up, and he peed all over my hands, so I quickly put him down and left him to do what toads do.

We came to the edge of the property line that bordered on Jackson Run Road and decided to cross it to get to the cornfield on the other side. As we walked, a big, fat groundhog darted, or should I say waddled, across the road right in front of us, heading back to his hole. "You know," Norma said, pointing to the groundhog, "my grandma and grandpa eat those guys. They say groundhogs are real tender and tasty."

That'll be the day, I thought to myself. *I'd really have to be starving.*

We continued up the small hill into the middle of the cornfield. It was late summer, and the husks were large with the silk tassels already turning brown. "I got a good idea, Jeannie," Norma said with a sly smile. "Why don't we pull off the brown cornsilk and make cigarettes we can smoke?"

"But we don't have any matches," I answered. "Why don't you run back to your grandma's house and find some matches we can use. Get some of that toilet paper in the outhouse, too."

"Okay, wait for me. I'll be right back," Norma said.

I plunked myself down in the middle of the field and waited for her. Ten minutes later, she returned, huffing and puffing from her run to and from the farmhouse. Norma was a chunky girl, not in the best physical shape, so that sprint almost did her in.

In between gasps, she said, "The only matches I could find were wooden house matches. These will have to do."

We went to work, pulling off the cornsilk and separating the drier, brown strands from the wet, white ones. After an hour or so, we laid out each square of toilet paper, ran a line of cornsilk down the length of the tissue, rolled it up and twisted the ends. They looked like cigarettes to us.

"Okay, Norma. Find a rock to strike the match and light yours," I said. She lit the make-shift cigarette. "Puff on it before the match goes out. Hurry."

Norma inhaled a lungful of smoke and coughed uncontrollably. "Boy, Jeannie, that's really strong. Look at it. The fire went out already."

"Let me try," I said. Between the white silk that was too moist and the afternoon breezes, the flame kept blowing out. I got a few mouthfuls of smoke, but we finally gave up after a half hour or more. Both of our throats were raw, and we smelled like a bonfire. We got back to the house just in time to climb into the car and head back home. Thankfully, Mr. and Mrs. Ellberg never noticed that we smelled like smoke.

NORMA AND I LOVED going to the movies on Saturday afternoons at the Columbia Theater on Second Street in Warren to see the serials. The Columbia was a great old theater; it had a balcony and a small stage up front where some famous people, including Hopalong Cassidy and his horse Topper, performed. Each week, we watched the next adventure of cowboys Roy Rogers, Gene Autry, the Lone Ranger, Hopalong Cassidy and Lash LaRue. One week, the featured film starred Lash LaRue, and we couldn't wait to see him capture more bad guys with his big bull whip. We bought our tickets and headed to the candy counter where I again bought my favorite, Good and Plenty; I loved those candy-coated licorice bits. Norma and I made our way to the balcony in the darkened theater and took our usual seats on the front row. From there, we looked down on the people below and locked in on targets for our candy wrapper and box missiles we flung over the railing if the movie got boring.

The newsreel was already running by the time we got there and was followed by a cartoon. I never understood why everyone laughed when a character was hit over the head, fell off a cliff, or got hurt in some way. Because of that, I only liked Pepe Le Pew cartoons. After the movie began, we ate our candy and sat glued to the screen; we never even thought about launching a surprise attack on the moviegoers below. Just when our hero was sure to die or the bad guy was getting away, the movie ended. We had to wait until the next week to see what happened.

Norma and I took our usual route home—east on Second Avenue, turned left on Market Street, passed the library and the Presbyterian Church to

Fourth Street where we walked along the railroad tracks to Fifth Street. That little section sat in the middle of thick woods, and we always imagined someone jumping out of the bushes to grab us. I never walked there alone. Sometimes we swore we heard *something* rattling around in the bushes and ran as fast as we could to get back out in the open. At other times, we had to scramble off the tracks when a train came through, blowing its plaintive whistle, alerting drivers to clear the tracks on Fourth and Fifth streets as it slowly chugged its way through town to the West End railroad station.

We turned east onto Fifth Avenue and crossed the bridge but not before we stared down in the muddy water, imagining what might be *lurking beneath the surface*. We had seen too many movies. At times, we saw large shapes in the water and knew it was the Loch Ness Monster that had found its way to Warren, Pennsylvania and lived under the bridge. We swore we saw giant carp and maybe even a musky or two; muskies, the common name for *muskellunge*, really did live there. They swam up the Allegheny River into the *crick*.

In no big hurry to return home, we made our way to Conewango Avenue, past the Beaty playground where we spent endless hours on the teeter-totters, monkey bars and swings, getting in a lively game of tetherball or making ourselves dizzy on the merry-go-round. On that day, we didn't stop to play but kept walking to Frank Street where I looked across the field and saw a horse grazing, a real horse. I knew it should not be there as the area was not fenced; the lot was bordered by houses on two sides, the *crick* in the back and the road up front.

"Look over there, Norma," I yelled. "It's a horse, and he's loose. He could get hit by a car. Wait for me; I'm going to get him." I crossed the street and casually walked toward him so as not to scare him. I reached down and picked a fistful of fresh grass and held it out to him. Luckily, he had on a halter, which I carefully took hold of and walked him across the field to the sidewalk where Norma was waiting. "Norma, run to the house next door and see if they have a rope I can use. If he gets spooked and rears up, I need something I can hold on to." I couldn't believe my good fortune, a real horse, just standing there waiting for me to find him. He wasn't the steed of my dreams; he was just a regular bay horse, but he was a living, breathing horse.

Norma returned a few minutes later with a piece of clothesline, which I tied to his halter and used to walk him down the sidewalk, clip-clopping all the way, music to my ears. "What are you going to do with him, Jean?"

"Why, I'm going to take him home and keep him," I said, looking at Norma like she was crazy for not knowing that. "I'll put him in the garage, and he

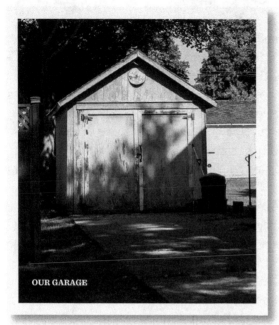

OUR GARAGE

can eat all the grass around our house then Daddy won't have to mow it anymore. Plus, Daddy will have all the manure he needs for his garden, and I'll have a horse I can ride anytime I want." I reached up and rubbed his neck. What more could any girl want?

I tied the horse to one of the maple trees in our front yard and ran into the house shouting, "I found a horse! I found a horse!"

"You what?" Mom asked as she walked to the front door and eyed my find. "Now, wait a minute, Jean. That is someone's horse. Don't you think they are going to be looking all over for him when they realize he's gone?"

"But, Mom, I found him. Finders keepers. Isn't that right? He's mine now."

"No, Jean, I'm sorry. That's not how it works," said Mom. "I'll call your father and see if he can find out who is the horse's owner." I heard her pick up the phone, and I went back outside to be with the horse. I scurried around for more fresh grass and picked some crabapples out back for him to snack on while I waited for someone to take my horse away. I waited and waited and hoped no one would ever come. Just then, an old pickup truck pulled up, and a man stepped out. He wore dirty overalls and had a cheek full of tobacco, which he spat out in between sentences.

"Yep, that's my horse all righty," the man drawled. "He knocked down a corner of the fence and just walked out into town." I didn't say anything. I just sat there and stared at the horse. "I thank ya for gettin' him for me, little lady. Here's a little something for yer trouble," he said, holding out a five-dollar bill. I just turned around and ran up the steps to my room and cried.

I didn't want five dollars; I wanted the horse. I did not understand why I couldn't have put him in the garage and kept him. Life was not fair. I swore that when I grew up I was going to have my own horse, and no one was ever going to take him away from me—ever, ever, ever!

New Member in the Family

IRIDE MY MAGNIFICENT black stallion to save the down trodden and rescue the weak from evil doers. I dig my heels into his flanks to spur him on, faster and faster, until his speed carries us high into the clouds to the beautiful blue skies, over mountains and lakes, ever faster until we reach our destination. His strength and power take my breath away. My spirit rises with every beat of his hooves. I smile into the ugly face of the danger that surrounds me. This is what I was born to do.

"JEAN, JEAN...time to get up for school," my mom yelled up the stairway. "You don't want to be late. Miss Erickson will give you a black mark." I lay in the bed, still groggy, trying to recapture my wonderful dream, so I could continue it with another chapter tonight when I went to sleep. I could do that. When I woke up before my dream was over, I picked it up where I left off the next time I went to sleep.

Pulling myself from the bed, I peered out my window into a cold, grey, Pennsylvania day. No sun, just grey. *Oh well, good day to be in school.* My bedroom was cold, so I hurried to the bathroom where a small, metal stove warmed the room and backed up close to the fire. I pulled out the hem of my nightgown and held it over the heater, trapping its warmth and defrosting my entire body. *Ahh...heaven.* After several minutes, I resigned myself to washing, brushing my teeth and dressing and then headed down to the kitchen for breakfast. My brother Donnie was already at the table, hunched over his toast and a bowl of cereal, devouring it as though he had not eaten in weeks. My older sister Kaye had already left for the day; she attended another school a mile away.

DONNIE AS A
YOUNG BOY

I looked over Donnie's shoulder into his bowl. My response to the contents always brought an audible aah or ooh if I liked what I saw or ick if it was the dreaded Ralston. I hated that cereal. It was gritty and tasted like dirt and was difficult to swallow. The only way to tolerate it at all was to smash as much of it as I could into my buttered toast and hide it there. *Thank you, Lord; it's not Ralston. It must be a cream of wheat or Quaker Oats morning.*

I looked around for Mom, but she wasn't there. Most mornings, she got up early with my dad, fixed his breakfast, packed his lunch, made our breakfast and put it in the double boiler to stay warm and went back to bed after we were all awake.

We had to wait until the weekend for the best breakfast of all—cocoa and buttered toast. On Saturdays when Mom slept in, Donnie and I mixed two teaspoons of cocoa, four teaspoons of sugar and two cups of milk in a saucepan and heated it. We poured this elixir into our cups and dunked three-quarters of a loaf of bread, toasted and slathered with butter, into this creamy, brown heaven. *Dunk, slurp, dunk, slurp...*the race was on to see who could eat the most toast in the shortest span of time. "C'mon Donnie, save some for me. You're such a pig!"

Donnie had freckles, curly brown hair, and the bluest-blue eyes that blazed when he got angry. He was only a year and a half older than I, so we competed in everything we did, even eating. We both wanted to be the best. Even though he was older, I was his protector, but it took me some time to prove it to him. Whenever I told him I was his defender, he got furious and beat me up.

My proof came the day a bully named Mark Mickleson decided to fight Donnie. I watched Donnie as he backed up and tried to get away. I stepped right up to Mark, stuck my jaw out, looked him straight in the eye and said, "Don't you touch my brother!" The bully was taken aback by my fierceness, and I saw fear in his eyes. He was a foot and a half taller than me, and even though I could have barely reached his chin with my fist, he gave it some thought, turned around and walked away. "Now Donnie, now do you believe I'm your protector?" He just shrugged and walked away.

AFTER WE FINISHED EATING a half loaf of bread, Donnie and I bundled up in our winter coats and walked the three blocks to school. "See you after school, Donnie. Let me know if you want me to help you with your paper route," I said as we parted ways at our classrooms.

Miss Erickson was my third grade teacher, and I had a crush on her. She was beautiful—tall and thin with dark brown, shoulder-length hair, glasses and pretty blue eyes. She spoke in a calm, quiet, yet authoritative voice and treated everyone with kindness, even the mischievous boys. I never saw her angry. She laughed easily but never at anyone, and she made learning fun. I arrived in class a few minutes early and put my lunch on the shelf in the coat closet. I pushed it as far back as I could in an attempt to protect it from the noon rush when everyone rifled through the bags, searching for their own or someone else's more appealing lunch. I took my seat, made sure my pencil was sharpened and that I had what I needed—books, crayons, scissors, paper, an eraser. Everything was ready.

Today was Tuesday, *goiter pill* day. I hated those goiter pills; they tasted terrible. What made those teachers think I was going to get a goiter? What the heck is a goiter anyway? None of that mattered. Every Tuesday, all the kids had to stand in line at the water fountain, and when my turn came, I had to take a drink of water, get the pill from Miss Erickson and swallow it, but I couldn't do it. Sometimes I sucked on it until it got smaller and smaller and finally disappeared, but I hated having that thing in my mouth for so long. The pill felt like small, hard granules of sand had been glued together, and it tasted like bad chocolate tinged with iodine. On other goiter-pill days, I waited until Miss Erickson wasn't looking, then I took the pill out of my mouth and threw it in the trash. *Yuk!*

After the class suffered through the goiter pill episode, we went on our weekly nature walk. "Okay children, get your coats out of the closet and bundle up. It's quite chilly outside," Miss Erickson said. Chaos prevailed as we all clamored to be the first kid out the door and into the crisp, cool air. "Stay in line and keep your eyes open for anything new and different we can all see," she directed.

We scrutinized everything. In the spring, we studied different kinds of ferns, dandelions, wildflowers, birds, bugs and bees. I especially liked those tiny, blue flowers we called *wet the beds*. We made it a game to see who could name all the plants, animals and insects we saw. I loved the outdoors and the smells of the wildflowers. During the fall and winter, we had to work much harder to find something interesting to examine. I enjoyed the musty smell of fallen leaves and watching the wind lift them off the ground and swirl them around in tight circles. Bugs fell from the trees, and the wrens chirped as they searched for seeds overlooked in previous weeks. Sometimes we wandered to the edge of the woods and found different varieties of moss and lichens on the trees and rocks. We found Christmas ferns, also called stocking ferns that looked like a holiday stocking.

Miss Erickson once instructed us to collect little plants and put them in a terrarium, water them, cover the container and watch the plants grow. My mom loaned me a large, clear casserole dish with a cover to use as my terrarium. Once I had it all set up, I put it on the dining room table next to the window. Watching the plants grow was okay, but then I got the bright idea to put in a caterpillar larva to see what would happen. After a month, the larva opened up and a little butterfly struggled to get out of its cocoon. I brought the terrarium outside, took the top off and let the butterfly go.

ON TODAY'S NATURE WALK, we explored for about an hour without seeing much, and then went back to our classroom for our mid-morning snack of a small bottle of never-perfect milk; it was always either warm or had frozen chunks floating around in it like little icebergs. *Disgusting!*

We started working on Halloween projects that afternoon. Miss Erickson passed out colored paper, and we traced ghoulish designs on the sheets. Then we used little scissors with rounded tips to cut out our witches, ghosts and pumpkins; I loved the crunching sound of scissors cutting through paper—*slice, slide, rip, slice, slide, rip*—and seeing the object's shape come to life.

The day went by fast and soon the bell rang, signaling the end of the school day. I grabbed my coat from the cloakroom and ran out the door to freedom. I couldn't wait to see what I had missed out in the world while being held captive in the classroom. The wind had picked up during the day, so I turned my collar up and tied my scarf tighter around my head to keep warm as I started down the street toward home.

Out of the corner of my eye, I saw movement in the bushes at one of the houses along the way. "What was that?" I asked myself out loud. I walked over to the bushes and peered down on a beautiful black and white puppy, lying in the dirt, looking up at me with soulful, brown eyes. It was shivering from the cold. "Oh, you poor thing. I wonder who you belong to." I stood around for a few minutes, deciding what to do. I had always wanted a dog of my own.

Then I remembered my sister Kaye's dog, a small, spotted-hound mix that had fits. My dad took it out in the backyard, tied it to the porch rail and shot it. His first shot missed and hit her collar, so the scared dog was running around loose in the yard. He shot again, and she fell over. He put her limp body in the garbage can to be hauled away in the morning. Kaye, Donnie and I sat on the stairs, listening to the shots and crying.

I certainly didn't want Dad to shoot this puppy. I knew I should walk away and leave the dog there, but I really wanted it to follow me home. *How could I get it to do that?* I had crackers in my pocket from some long-ago snack. "Are you hungry, little dog? Want a cracker?" I said, as I tossed a piece of cracker to the puppy. It worked! She came out of the bushes and grabbed the cracker. Then I got a good look at the most beautiful, little dog I had ever seen. She had short hair with a black head and black saddle and black and white spots everywhere else. She could not have weighed more than ten pounds. I fell in love; I just knew this was the dog for me. I coaxed her all the way home with bits of stale crackers while I thought about where I could hide her, so Mom and Dad wouldn't find her until I made my case. I also didn't want her to run away during the night.

When I got home, I decided to hide her in the garage where no one would see her. I rooted through my dad's garden tools, our bicycles and sleds and found a long box with an open end that worked perfectly. She'd stay warm in the closed-up box. I put an old towel in the box for her to sleep on, and then enticed her into her little house with the rest of the crackers.

"Hi Mom, I'm home," I yelled out as I walked into the back door. "Boy, I'm hungry. Guess I'll have a peanut butter and jelly sandwich, okay?" No answer. Mom was in the other room doing something, so I quietly opened the refrigerator door to see what we had that the puppy could eat. *Hmmmmm...lookee here, a piece of meat with some fat on it. No one will miss it.* I stashed it into my coat pocket, and quickly opened the garage door and tossed the piece of meat into the puppy's box before heading back into the house. I needed some time to think about how to handle this situation. Back in the house, I picked up a book and tried to look like I was reading while I devised a scheme.

Meanwhile, Dad came home from work, and shortly thereafter, Donnie finished his paper route, put his bike in the garage and discovered the puppy. "Mom, Dad, there's a dog in the garage. What's it doing there?" Donnie yelled out.

Oh oh, now I'm in trouble.

"Jean, do you know anything about a dog in the garage?" Mom asked.

"Well, uh, yeah. The dog followed me home from school. She was so cute; I didn't want her to freeze, so I put her in the garage."

"All right, but she can't stay out there," Mom said. "Bring her in the house where she'll be warm. We will find out who she belongs to tomorrow."

Yes, now we're talking! I knew that once I got her in the house, everyone was going to fall in love with her like I did. After I brought her in, Mom and Dad looked her over and petted her a little bit. I could tell they were taken with her, too.

Mom looked up from the dog and said, "Jean, go to the store and get her a can of dog food. I'm sure she's hungry."

I grabbed my coat and raced out the door, down one block to Churchill's Grocery Store, bought the food and made it back to the house within five minutes. I opened the can and gave her the whole thing. She devoured it within minutes and then went and lay on the couch next to Mom. *Good move, little dog. Now you're thinking.*

The next thing I knew, the puppy up-chucked all her dinner right beside Mom on the sofa. *That did it. They are going to toss her out for sure now.*

"Jean, come clean this up," Mom said. She wasn't even mad. I did as I was told then came and sat on the sofa next to the puppy. I studied her closely, picking the perfect name for her. I didn't have to think too hard. Spot, of course. *My* dog's name was Spot.

After supper, it was time for bed and to return to my dream of protecting the world as I rode my beautiful steed with a little black and white dog named Spot running beside us.

All Mine

JEAN, JEAN, TIME TO GET UP," Mom called up to me. "You have a puppy to get outdoors. She's down here whining."

Groggy for sleep, it took me a minute to realize where I was and that the noise I heard was Mom. I looked at the clock next to the bed. I barely made out the numbers through my heavy-lidded, bleary eyes. Six o'clock in the morning, still dark outside. I bailed out of bed, threw on my jeans and sweater and ran down the stairs to meet a wagging tail and two, big, brown eyes, looking up at me. I truly was in love.

I grabbed my winter coat and called to Spot as I ran out the side door, slamming it behind me. The air felt cold and crisp, and except for the streetlight shining at the corner, I couldn't make out much in the dark. Spot stayed close by my side and sniffed around, deciding where she wanted to deposit her gift to the outside world. She already seemed to be housebroken, no accidents during the night. Spot was perfect.

Because of the cold, Spot didn't waste any time, and we rushed back into the warm house. I hoped to get into the bathroom and get ready first this morning, so I'd have more time to play with Spot before school, but my older sister Kaye beat me to it. I waited quietly, trying not to wake up Donnie and Linda, so I'd be next. I wanted to get in every second of play time with Spot; I was so afraid someone would claim her while I was in class. I didn't want to give her back.

Eventually, we all made it to the kitchen and sat down to a breakfast of yucky, cooked Ralston and toast. It was gritty in my mouth and had big lumps because Mom didn't stir it enough. We all despised that breakfast, but Mom bought into the endorsement of cowboy, radio and film star Tom Mix who claimed Ralston was great for growing kids. After I forced down the last bite, I petted Spot one last time and prayed that the person who owned her didn't ever want her back.

Mom had already begun her weekly ironing. Tuesday was ironing day. I kissed her on the lips and *zap*. She got me again. Every time our lips touched when Mom was ironing, I got shocked. Every Tuesday! I hated that feeling, but I never remembered it from one week to the next.

All day long, I thought about Spot. Daddy promised he'd ask everyone at the post office where he worked if they knew who the puppy belonged to. I couldn't focus on my schoolwork; my mind kept drifting back to Spot and praying that her owners somehow knew she belonged with me. This felt like the longest day of my life.

Finally the bell rang. I grabbed my coat and flew out the door, running down the street as fast as I could. I opened the door, and there was Spot, waiting for me. She wagged her whole body, not just her tail. I bent down to pick her up, and she kissed me all over my face and wiggled around like she couldn't get close enough. "Have you heard anything, Mom?"

"No, not yet, Jean. We'll have to wait for your dad to get home."

I played ball with Spot until she got tired, then I held her as she napped, counting the minutes until Daddy came home. Finally at 5:30 p.m., the door opened, and my daddy walked in. I didn't even wait for him to take off his coat. "Did you find out anything? Anything at all?" I peppered him with questions.

He stood in the doorway with his hands in his pockets and gave me a solemn look. I held my breath as I tried to read the look on his face. *I know it. I know he found the owner, and they want their puppy back, just like the man who took away the horse I found. I just know it! Please, please, please don't let him tell me that.* I wrapped my arms around Spot and stared at my dad, waiting for him to say something, anything.

"Well, Jean," he said and then paused. His face was blank. "I did find out who owns the dog." My heart pounded in my chest. *And...and?* "Yes, I talked to the people who Spot belongs to..." He glanced away for a second or two. "They said the dog I described was indeed theirs," he said, taking a breath between each word, "but the dog kept running away. They don't want her and said you can have her."

What? Did he just say what I thought he said? She's mine? Spot understood. She started licking my face and arms. I ran to my dad and hugged him tight while Spot smothered him in thank you licks. *You're mine, Spot, all mine.*

Where Babies Come from

SPOT WASN'T AN ORDINARY DOG. She was my constant companion, a fellow adventurer, my protector, and my entertainer for eleven years. She will always be one of the smartest animals I've ever known. Sometimes I wonder how differently my life might have turned out if I had not found her that day in the bushes when she was only four or five months old. Dad figured her to be half beagle, which gave her an incredible sense of smell, and half fox terrier, which made her very intelligent.

Spot and I played a game in the house when no one else was home. I took cheese out of the refrigerator and cut it into small pieces. Then I made Spot sit in a chair in the living room while I hid cheese bites all over the house. When finished, I told her, "Go find the cheese, Spot. Go get it!" Off she went. She put her nose to the floor and ran all around the downstairs, rooting out bits of cheese from my best hiding places. She gobbled up each treat and eyed me with such a satisfied look on her face while waiting for me to confirm what she already knew—she was a really good dog.

Whenever we had company, Spot took center stage. I showed everyone how she could heel, speak, sneeze, say her prayers,

SPOT SITTING UP AND BEGGING

shake hands, crawl, roll over, play dead, leap through my arms, jump and put her paws on my shoulders while I held her in my arms, and climb ladders and trees in her pursuit of squirrels.

AMONG HER MANY OTHER TALENTS, Spot was a professional beggar and made the rounds to all the neighbors almost every morning, looking for scraps. She first stopped at the Budds' house and scratched at the backdoor. If Mrs. Budd had any leftovers from the night before, she opened the door and put out a dish for Spot. Spot then visited the Boyds and the Campbells, who always had a handout for her.

When the neighbors weren't around, Spot helped herself to whatever she found. The Bidwells sometimes left ears of corn still in the husks on the back porch. Spot held the corn with her paws, pulled off the husks with her teeth and settled in to enjoy some fresh corn on the cob. At first, I didn't believe Spot could manage that, but Mr. Bidwell said he saw her steal the corn and shuck and eat it while he watched out his back window.

Spot wasn't hungry; she just liked to beg. I think it was a game for her to see if she could get something out of the neighbors. I fed Spot Gro-Pup Dog Food every night. I lay on the kitchen floor and handed her the ribbon dry dog food one at a time because I loved to hear her crunch. Sometimes when I got busy with drawing or reading and forgot to give Spot her supper, she let us know. Dad would yell up to me, "Jean, Spot's pestering me. Did you feed her tonight?" She never missed a meal.

BUT SPOT'S BEST TRICK OF ALL, which she saved for only me, was going deaf when she was in season and running off with her suitors. She didn't even hear my screams as she streaked off with the male she fancied at that moment.

One Saturday morning before I understood anything about the birds and bees, Mom asked me to go to Churchill's Grocery and pick up a loaf of bread. "Jean, please put Spot on a leash and don't let any dogs near her."

"No problem, Mom," I answered as I put the collar around Spot's neck and ran out the back door. On the way to the store, I noticed Yank, a little tri-colored, male fox terrier, following us at a distance. He was too far for me to chase away but close enough to pick up Spot's scent. Somehow the leash got tangled up, and I stopped to undo the knot. When I looked back at Spot, she and Yank were attached end to end. I didn't know what to do. I panicked, dropped the leash and ran the one and a half blocks to my house. I threw open the side door and yelled at my mother, "The dogs are stuck together; the dogs are stuck together!" This was terrible. I just knew they were going to die.

"Oh, my," my mother answered. "Now we're going to have puppies."

Puppies? Surely Spot was being killed by that other dog. I couldn't understand how Spot being in that terrible situation could produce puppies. Obviously, I knew nothing about where puppies came from, but if Spot wasn't being killed and puppies were the result, maybe that horrible scene wasn't so bad after all. "Okay, Mom. I have to go find her. She still has the leash on," I said.

Mom was right. Nine weeks later, Spot gave birth to four roly-poly puppies.

JEAN AND SPOT'S PUPPY, PANDY

We prepared a box for her to raise her little ones on the landing approaching the cellar. For six weeks, she cleaned and fed and took good care of her babies. Spot allowed anyone to hold her puppies, except Johnnie Bidwell. Johnnie lived next door and was my sister's age. He teased Spot all the time, and Spot wouldn't forget it. She'd bite Johnnie in a second when he tried to touch her puppies.

I spent every free moment with Spot and her puppies. Because Dad worked in the post office, he saw everyone in town and quickly found good homes for all our *little Spots*. I hated to see them go, but we gave them away as soon as they were old enough to be away from their mother. Spot was ready; she was tired of being a mom.

SPOT'S ADVENTURES in reproduction played out once or twice every year, much to my dismay. One spring, I looked out the front window and saw a pack of seven or eight dogs, lying there waiting for their next conquest to begin. Mostly it was a civil gathering, but at times, one dog walked up to another, stood over him with his hackles raised and teeth bared, begging for a fight. The lowly dog cowered until his attacker walked away. None of the dogs ever gave up and went home. They all thought persistence paid off, and they would be the lucky dog of the day.

Smokey was the most obnoxious dog of the pack. A cross between a setter and some type of hound, he had a long tail, somewhat long ears and was a muddy brown and gray color. He lived up the block, so he was usually first on the scene every season. For a solid week, he *never* left our yard. He grew skinny because he didn't even leave to eat. Smokey continued his vigil, night and day, knowing his perseverance would surely pay off. And it did. Someone opened the door, and Spot shot out, and when I finally caught up with her, she and Smokey were doing the deed in the middle of Conewango Avenue, oblivious to the traffic going around them. The people in the cars pointed and laughed, and I felt so embarrassed. I hated that dog Smokey. He was such a bad influence on Spot.

At times when Spot wasn't nearby, Smokey tried to mount me. I guess he figured I smelled like Spot, so if she wasn't around, I'd do. I hated that dog.

During another one of Spot's amorous times, I tried to squeeze out the door and not let her out, but she slipped through my legs, pushed open the screen door, ran down the steps and headed up Kenmore Street. Her seven suitors were up and racing down the street behind Spot.

"Dad, Dad," I shouted, "Spot's run off with the dogs. Help me catch her."

Dad jumped out of his chair and ran with me down Kenmore Street and Conewango Avenue. We must have looked like quite a sight—Spot leading the parade with her head up and tail wagging, followed by seven dogs then me, then Dad. We ended our pursuit a block or two later as Dad and I gasped for breath and stared at the dogs as they disappeared around the curve. Spot didn't come home until the next day. She was dirty and tired, but she had a very satisfied look on her face. Nine weeks later, we had four more beautiful pups to give away.

I KNEW NOTHING about where puppies came from until I saw Spot end to end with the neighbor dog that first time. *What about babies? When I get married and my husband and I decide to have a baby, do we have to get stuck together? That is disgusting! What if we are in a hotel, and there is a fire? We'll get burned up and die! No way!*

Over the years, I had asked my mother several times where babies came from, but she always answered, "Not now, Jean. I have the book put away somewhere. I'll find it when I have a minute and show you." *What book?* I never saw any book or had that conversation, so I learned everything on my own, from girlfriends mostly.

One day as Janet and I walked down a dirt road next to the woods, I looked down and spotted something that looked like a half deflated balloon. "Look, Janet, a balloon," I said. "I'm going to blow it up."

I reached down to pick up the balloon, and Janet screamed at me. "Don't touch it, Jeannie, don't touch it." I asked her why not, and she said, "Men use those when women have diseases, and they don't want to catch them."

I couldn't believe what I was hearing. If what Janet said was true, that was gross. "Are you lying to me, Janet? I don't believe it. You're always trying to make me believe stupid stuff," I said. Janet looked at me with a smug, knowing expression that said how stupid I was. I dropped the subject. I did not want to know anything else about sex.

Gayle

GAYLE'S DESK SAT NEXT TO MINE in our first grade classroom at Home Street School. Her last name was Branch, so when the teacher arranged our class alphabetically, we sometimes sat in desks next to each other. We played during recess and often walked home together because she lived only a couple of blocks from me. Gayle was easy going and fun to be with, and we became fast friends.

Her dark, curly hair fell to her shoulders and the perky, turned up smile she always wore made her look very Irish; she was at least half Irish. The friendship Gayle and I shared followed us through our school years, and we spent a great deal of time together, especially when I was fighting with Janet. Janet and I played well when we were together, and Gayle and I got along great when it was just us. Add the third girl into the mix, and invariably one of us went home mad at the other two.

At the time, Gayle was the oldest of four children. She

JEAN, GAYLE AND NORMA

had two younger sisters—Tippy and Margo—and one little brother Jeff; another brother, Randy, was born a few years later. With all those kids making messes, Gayle had many chores to do after school and during the summer. I spent a lot of time sitting and watching her clean the house, wash dishes, iron, and do whatever else she needed to while her mother worked at the state hospital.

Often I called her in the morning and asked if she could come out and play; her usual response was, "Not until I get my jobs done. Why don't you come over and keep me company?" Spot and I walked over to her house. Spot lay on the front porch and slept until it was time to go, which was often hours later. I helped her sometimes, so we could get outside and play sooner.

We usually ended up in the basement where one side of the room was set up for entertaining with an old couch, a couple of chairs, and a record player. In a separate room, an ironing board was set up, waiting for Gayle. She ironed for hours while I sat in a straight-backed chair across from her and chatted while she worked. Thankfully, her mother never made her use the *mangle;* it was one scary looking machine. It had two big rollers into which her mother fed clean sheets, pillowcases, tablecloths, napkins, and such, anything flat. On the other side, the linens came out pressed and wrinkle-free. I could see why they called it a *mangle,* because it could definitely mangle someone. I imagined Gayle's fingers getting caught in that beast and it pulling the rest of her through its rollers, sending her out the other side as flat as a paper doll.

SOMETIMES GAYLE asked me to sleep over on Saturday night; we always had fun, and they had a lot of snacks to eat. Gayle's father, Mr. Branch, worked at Anderson's Bakery, and every night he brought home bread, rolls, cupcakes, and lots of doughnuts he removed from the grocery shelves because they were expired. I never understood how a doughnut expired, but having all those sweets made breakfast exciting at Gayle's house.

Every morning, Gayle's brother and sisters rushed through the kitchen door all at the same time, pushing and shoving, trying to be first to pile into the breakfast nook and gorge on the doughnuts and rolls. They were like vacuum cleaners that sucked up everything in sight. I was lucky to grab one whole doughnut before all that was left was a pile of crumbs and spilled milk that Gayle patiently cleaned up after the locusts left the table. I didn't have that kind of tolerance; I would have smacked those little monsters upside the head until they behaved.

One thing no one fought for was the so-called *butter* from the refrigerator. It consisted of a bag of white lard called *oleo.* Inside the bag was a little orange ball that you squeezed to make the oleo yellow, so it looked like butter. I liked to squeeze the little ball, but I just couldn't eat the stuff. My dad said all the time, "I don't care how poor we are, we're going to have lots of milk and real butter in our house." If I ate toast at Gayle's house, I piled on the peanut butter and jelly instead of that awful oleo.

Bonnie was also a member of the Branch family. She was a St. Bernard, a huge brown and white dog with a black mask and eyes with sagging lower lids. For Mrs. Branch, it was love at first sight. She loved Bonnie from the moment she laid eyes on her, so the big dog came home to live with them. Bonnie was a friendly dog and liked everyone, and I liked her, but I stayed away from her mouth. Six-inch-long strings of drool hung from her mouth, clinging to everything it touched, so I made sure I wasn't a receptacle for her slobber. When I even *thought* she might be winding up to shake her head, I backed up at least five feet to stay out of the spray.

Bonnie ran away all the time. Really I should say *walked* away, because I never saw her run anywhere. She just lumbered along, getting where she wanted to be eventually. At least once a week, she'd take off and later be picked up by the Warren Police Department and brought back home. She was the only St. Bernard in town, so they knew where she belonged. Many times, I saw the patrol car pull up out front of the Branches' house, and there was Bonnie, sitting in the back seat, drooling, looking out the window and enjoying the ride.

One day while at Gayle's house, I saw one of the local dogs mounting Bonnie. She was in season and tied to the garage door. I screamed for Mr. Branch, and he ran out the door with a pail, filled it up with water and doused the two dogs. That quickly solved the problem; the terrified suitor ran off and disappeared into the neighborhood. Eventually Bonnie went to live on a farm, which was a much more appropriate place for a huge, slobbery dog like her.

GAYLE DIDN'T SHOW UP at school one day, and I called her when I got home. "Gayle, were you sick today?" I asked.

"No, I had to stay at home and watch the kids. Mom and Dad had to take Jeff to the hospital for a mastoid operation," she replied.

"A mastoid operation. What's that?"

"He had this big lump behind his ear, and they had to take it out."

As soon as I hung up, I put my fingers behind my ears and checked to see if I had any lumps. I found a small bump in back of my left ear and was sure it was going to turn into mastoiditis, and I'd need an operation. For years, I checked behind my ear several times every day and slept only on my left side.

ONE MORNING in late summer, the phone rang, and it was Gayle. "What are you doing today, Jean?" she asked.

FRIENDS GAYLE AND JANET

"Oh, nothing special. Do you want to go to the *prairie* and play horses?"

Gayle put her hand over the mouthpiece, but I could still hear her asking her mom if she could go. "Yeah, Jean, I can go. See you in a little while."

I told Mom where I was going, took the stairs two at a time up to my room to change into my clean jeans and cowboy shirt, ran back down to the kitchen, packed some peanut butter and jelly sandwiches, then headed out the door and up the street. Halfway there, I remembered the matches and knife I wanted to bring along in case I needed it. I dug deep into my pocket and felt something strange, definitely not matches and a knife. They were stringy, long pieces of something. I pulled the bits out of my pocket to find dried up worms. I had put the very-much-alive worms in my pocket last time I went fishing, and apparently, Mom washed my jeans and hung them up on the line to dry. Yuck! I threw the worm pieces on the ground and found the matches and my knife in the other pocket.

WHEN I GOT TO GAYLE'S, I had to wait for her to finish up one more job, and then we ran out the house before her mother thought of something else that needed to be done. Gayle told me that she had called Janet and told her what we were doing. Janet said she'd come meet us later. "Aww, Gayle. Now, why did you invite her?" I said.

"I don't know," she replied with a shrug.

"You know how Janet is. She always causes trouble before the day's over," I said.

We dropped the subject of Janet and talked about other things as we walked up Conewango Avenue to Quaker Hill Road in back of the *Old Ladies Home,* as we called Watson Memorial Home, to the prairie, which was a huge, flat area that used to be Warren Fairgrounds. Way back when, they had fairs and horse races there, watched by lots of people who sat in a large grandstand.

This was the perfect day to be at the fairgrounds. It was warm and bright with large, fluffy, white clouds that shielded us from the direct sunlight, so we didn't get too hot running all around the open area. "Okay, Jean, what's your name?" Gayle asked as we began playing horses.

"I'll be Midnight," I answered. "I'm a stallion, and you can be my mare. I'll round you up and save you from the bad guys."

"I'll be Stormy," Gayle said, and we galloped all over our prairie until we ran out of breath and found a shady place to rest and cool off.

AFTER TAKING A BREATHER, I said to Gayle, "Let's go up the hill and see if we can find any wild blueberries to eat." We walked through the lush grass in search of some elusive berries; the bushes were small and hidden by the tall grass. For a half hour, we filled up on tiny, sweet berries and then ate our peanut butter and jelly sandwiches. Full and happy, Gayle and I plopped down on our backs on a grass-covered hill and looked up at the blue sky, making up silly names for the clouds and giggling.

"Jeannie, Gayle, where are you?" Janet, the troublemaker, looked all around the pasture for us.

"We're up here, Janet," Gayle answered. We sat up and watched as Janet climbed the hill to meet us. Then we began talking about what to do next.

"I know what we can do," I said. "Let's go over to the woods across the way and build a shack. I'm sure there's a lot of dead wood we can use."

"That sounds fun. Let's go," Gayle said.

We walked across the hill into the trees and searched around for the right spot to build our shack. The woods were on an incline, so we had to find a fairly level area with four trees close enough to each other for us to build the cabin walls but far enough away for us to have some room inside.

Finally, we found just the right spot. Then we took dead, straight limbs, some almost too heavy to drag, and placed them on the outside of the trees, making a log cabin. We left an opening for the door and built a roof with smaller limbs and covered it with leaves.

"Are we almost done?" Janet whined. "I'm hot and tired."

"C'mon Janet, just think how neat this place will be when we get done. Our own little shack," I said. She wasn't impressed, so I kept trying. "We can come up here and have picnics and make a fire all by ourselves. We can even bring breakfast and fry bacon and eggs." She reluctantly went back to work.

All afternoon, we dragged limbs to build our shack, and once we put on the last branch, we sat on the hill and admired our work. "Hey Janet," I said, "your face is all dirty."

"Real funny, Jeannie. So is yours and so is Gayle's," Janet said. We looked around at each other and laughed at how filthy we all were.

After resting for a bit, I got the bright idea that we needed a patio to sit on and a rock fireplace to light and keep us warm when the weather cooled down. A great deal of shale lay under the carpet of dried leaves, covering the woodsy hillside, so we used small pieces of shale for digging, to make the space level, and then we put the bigger pieces on top, ending up with a patio approximately six by ten feet. We made a fireplace with the remaining pieces of shale.

We scurried around, finding bits of wood to use for our fire. It was already late afternoon, and Gayle had to be home by five o'clock. I used the matches I brought to light the tinder. Crouching in a circle around the fireplace, we blew on the tinder until the fire started then put heavier pieces of wood on top to make the blaze larger. Finally the fire ignited, and we sat back on our little patio, watching the peaceful scene and enjoying our efforts until *kaboom!* The entire fireplace exploded and threw hot, fiery pieces of wood up in the air in an eight-foot circle around us.

We stood there in stunned silence for a minute or two. *My God, what have we done?* "We got to get this fire out, or it's going to set the woods on fire," I yelled. Tiny pieces of ignited wood settled everywhere beneath the dry leaves. The only way we found them was by looking for the small tendrils of smoke and the open fires. We worked furiously to stamp out all the fires around us, but it was a waiting game to see where it was going to ignite next.

"Well, I have to go home now," Janet said.

"What? You can't go now," I said. "You have to stay with us, so we can make sure all the fires are out. If we don't, the woods will catch on fire." If looks killed, Janet would be dead with the dirty look I shot off in her direction.

"Nope, got to go home. See ya," Janet said, and off she went. *What a mean little kid. She doesn't think of anybody but herself.*

Five o'clock came, and Gayle faced sure punishment for coming home late. *Please God, don't leave me alone here to make sure the fire is out.* Gayle eased my mind and said, "I'll stay, Jean, until we make sure all the fire is out. I won't leave you here by yourself." That was why I loved her so much; she was a true friend. We waited another half hour until we felt fairly certain we had put out all the live embers, and then we left for home.

An hour after I got home and took a bath to get all the grime off of me, I went downstairs to watch Mom fix dinner. "Where were you all day today, Jean?" she asked.

"I thought I told you this morning...Janet, Gayle and I spent the day in the woods," I answered. "Boy, am I ever hungry. What's for dinner?"

Just then the phone rang; it was Gayle. "Jean, guess what? The woods are on fire. The fire trucks just raced by my house. I looked out the window on the stairs, and I can see the fire from here. My mom told me I couldn't leave the house."

"Mom, Mom, there's a fire in the woods. Can I go see it?" I asked.

"No Jean. Stay right here," she answered. "You don't have any business being there."

The next evening the *Warren Times Mirror* newspaper came out, and I couldn't resist. In the Daily Happenings section, there it was—an article about a fire in the woods behind the Old Ladies Home. The fire burned an acre of ground before the fire department could put out the blaze. They attributed the fire to a hobo, staying in the woods, because of all the whiskey and beer bottles laying around. No one ever found out the truth.

Uncle Don and Uncle Glenn

MY MOTHER'S YOUNGER BROTHERS, Don and Glenn Ecklund, were military men and chose to spend their leaves at our house. Uncle Don was in the U.S. Coast Guard and Uncle Glenn, a chief petty officer and career Navy man. We knew of their visits only a week in advance, and I counted the days to their arrival. If I wasn't in school, I sat at the front window and looked for them. From the minute they arrived to the time they left, our house was filled with laughter and jokes, fun times and excitement. I liked my mother's two older sisters, Vera and Ruth, but I adored my Uncle Don and Uncle Glenn. When either of them came to visit, we never knew what to expect next.

I asked each of them the same question as soon as they walked in the door, "When are you leaving?"

Uncle Glenn always responded, "Do you want me to leave already? I just got here, Jean."

"No, no, no...but when are you leaving?" I answered. I wanted to know exactly how long they were staying, so I wouldn't be so disappointed when they left. I needed to know, so I could count the days and enjoy my uncles to the fullest because I knew I wouldn't see them again for a whole year. While in our home, I followed them wherever they went. Once I even walked in on Uncle Don in the bathroom. He had to circle around the commode to retain his privacy.

Uncle Don stood six feet tall, was thin with a dark complexion, dark hair and a stylish mustache that accentuated a smile of shiny, white teeth. The sparkle in his deep brown eyes told me that a joke was never far off. Uncle Glenn was Mom's youngest brother, and like Uncle Don, he was six-

UNCLE DON ECKLUND

feet tall and square jawed, but he was clean shaven. I thought they were the most handsome men I had ever seen. Single and in their late twenties, both my uncles were jokesters and loved making people laugh. Some of the jokes they told when they *thought* I was out of earshot were the ones I memorized and recounted at inappropriate times.

The way Uncle Don shaved fascinated me. Every morning, he carried his little black, leather shaving bag into the bathroom, put it on the back of the commode and set his straight razor on the sink. He took out a wooden lather cup or shaving mug, which already had hard soap in the bottom. Then he added few drops of water to the cup and used a small brush to really work up a stiff lather. When he had enough foam, he wet his face and then proceeded to cover everything from the tops of his cheeks down to his neck with thick suds. Sometimes he put shaving cream on the end of my nose just to make me laugh.

Uncle Don picked up the razor, slowly ran it across his skin, making a scratching sound, and then flipped the foam and little bits of black whiskers into the sink. He repeated the same process, stroke by stroke, across his entire face and had to go over most spots more than once because of his heavy beard. When he came to his mustache, he held up his nose with one finger of his left hand and carefully circled his mustache, then ran the razor up and down his neck, making sure he did not nick his Adam's apple. He didn't often cut himself, but when he did, he used a septic stick to stop the bleeding. To finish up, Uncle Don cupped his hands under the faucet and splashed clean water onto his face to get rid of the remaining shaving foam then gently slapped his neck and cheeks with an aftershave lotion, maybe Old Spice. I felt like I had a front-row seat at a show. What a magnificent performance! For an encore, he allowed me to touch his smooth face. I watched him shave every day he let me.

AT SOME POINT while in the Coast Guard, Uncle Don spent time in Hawaii and surprised with a hula skirt outfit, complete with a little top, leis, ankle bracelets and thongs for my feet. I paraded around my neighborhood most of the summer in my Hawaiian-girl getup, letting my long hair loose and flowing down my back. All day, I dreamed about going to Hawaii and living in my hula skirt. Two years later, he sent me another outfit; the first one fell apart because I wore it so much.

Uncle Don came to visit the fall after I got Spot, and he liked to take her squirrel and rabbit hunting with him. Spot enjoyed it, too, and put her whole heart into the task. She chased every squirrel and rabbit in sight, so much so that at times she overran the animal and lost the prey. At the end of a day of hunting with Uncle Don, Spot came home so lame, she could barely walk.

JEAN IN HER HULA SKIRT - 1940

Uncle Don used a shotgun because he didn't like to miss. He proudly brought home his kill and went down into the basement to cut and clean the squirrels and rabbits. Even though she was exhausted, Spot crawled down the stairs to join him and claim her reward—the hearts and livers of the animals she chased and Uncle Don killed.

My mother dutifully dusted the fallen beasts in flour and fried them in a large cast iron skillet with Crisco. Once they were browned, she turned down the heat, put a lid on the pan and let the poor creatures simmer. She served the pitiful platter of scrawny squirrels and rabbits to our family with mashed potatoes, canned green beans and applesauce, and I could tell Uncle Don felt good about bringing home dinner for his family. It was a delicious meal, but we had to deal with so many bones. Beyond that, someone always ended up spitting out the BBs lodged in the meat.

HULA GIRL

UNCLE DON CAME AND SPENT Christmas with us one year when I was six or seven years old. While Mom and Dad went into town for some last-minute purchases, they asked Uncle Don to keep an eye on us. He thought about what he could do to keep three little kids occupied for a few hours and got a bright idea. "Hey kids, let's surprise Mom and Dad and hang some popcorn garlands on the tree." We always decorated our tree a night or two before Christmas Eve, so this would be a good way to get started.

My sister Kaye got needles and thread out of Mom's sewing bag while Uncle Don popped the corn. He sat us down in a circle on the floor, put a huge dish of popcorn in the middle and handed us the needles strung with long, double-stranded thread. We were excited and ready to get started on this fun task. But the kernels of popcorn kept breaking, causing us to prick our fingers with the needle. We kept trying, but the popcorn must have been old and stale, and it just would not stay together.

"Ouch, ouch...this hurts," Donnie cried.

"I don't like this; it's no fun," I whined. Kaye sat there and said nothing, but her twisted-up face told me she was trying to keep from crying.

Uncle Don tried to keep our spirits up by telling us, "Just think what a surprise it will be for your mom and dad when they come home and see how pretty the tree is all wrapped in strings of popcorn."

We kept trying, but hours later, we had very little popcorn on our strings. Most of it was broken and strewn on the floor all around us. We heard the front door open; Mom and Dad were here to save us. They walked into the living room and took one look at popcorn scattered everywhere, our pathetic faces that were full of tears, and Uncle Don trying to keep a straight face; he found the situation hilarious but didn't dare laugh.

My parents tried to look concerned and keep their composure, but their contorted faces ended up in comical smiles. Dad came to the rescue and suggested that maybe we were tired and ought to go to bed. They would finish the job. This was the first time I was actually glad to go to bed early, so I could nurse my sore fingertips. I never tried to string popcorn again.

UNCLE DON'S BRIGHT IDEAS like making popcorn garland went back to his days as a kid. Mom told me about a time when she, Uncle Glenn and Uncle Don sat around the table, eating a box of Nabisco saltine crackers. No doubt they were bored and decided to see who could stuff the most crackers into his or her mouth. That was going along okay until nine-year-old Uncle Don decided to put the two-inch square cracker into his mouth without breaking it. He stretched his mouth wide and eased the cracker in. "Ook, ook, I did it," he mumbled. My mother reached over and pushed the cracker deep into Uncle Don's mouth with the flat of her hand and split both corners of his mouth. Mom and Uncle Glenn looked at each other and roared with laughter. Something about Don's mishap touched off their Swedish sense of humor.

UNCLE DON LOVED TO PARTY, which sometimes involved tipping the bottle just enough to make him unsteady on his feet. Since we were quite young at the time, we went to bed early and missed most of the fun. One evening, Uncle Don went out with his friends, and our family went to bed. Sometime in the early morning hours, we all awoke to a resounding crash and someone rolling down a flight of stairs, then complete silence. I bolted upright in my bed, scared by the loud noise and wondering if we had a burglar in the house. I held my breath for a few seconds, and then heard this loud, booming voice I knew so well, "Who put the goddamned marbles on the stairs?"

UNCLE GLENN ECKLUND

LIKE UNCLE DON, Uncle Glenn was known to have a few too many at times. One afternoon, I came home from playing outside and walked in the front door to find Uncle Glenn lying on his side on the living room floor next to a little gas stove we used to heat the room. He rested his head on one hand, and apparently, his eyes weren't focusing because he kept reaching out to one column on the stove, thinking it was a bottle of beer.

"*Ish my boddle. Gimme my beer. I can't reash my boddle,*" he slurred, and then he began to sing:

Kith me onth and kith me twith,
then kith me onth again.
Ith been a wong, wong time.

Haven't felt like thith before,
Thinth can't remember when.
Ith been a wong, wong time.
Oh yeah!

I STOOD THERE A FEW MINUTES, staring down at him, not knowing what to think. When I recovered from the shock of seeing him in that condition, I went into the kitchen to ask my mom and dad what they were going to do with Uncle Glenn. Dad just looked at me and smiled, "Just leave him alone for a while; we'll put him to bed soon. He had just a little too much libation," which I figured was another word for beer.

THE PARTY STARTED at our house when either of my uncles walked in the door. Daddy's side of the family was pretty stuffy and weren't drinkers, so when Uncle Don or Uncle Glenn came to town, Dad let go for a bit, enjoyed a few drinks and some fun.

One summer weekend, Uncle Glenn and our family went on a picnic to War Pen, a park outside of Warren. Dad especially loved these picnics. He grilled the hotdogs and the hamburgers, and everyone sat around, caught up and drank beer.

Uncle Glenn knew how much I loved horses, so he rented us each one from the stables at the park. That was the weekend I met Cotton and fell in love for the first time. Cotton was a white, part-Arabian pony with a long mane and tail who was a retired circus horse. He was a real show horse. I learned that if I pulled on the reins just a little, he reared up just like he used to do in the ring.

The weekend riders traveled single file on a path through the woods and fields beside a stream, and we could trot or lope our horses for short distances. Uncle Glenn and I stayed at the back of line, so I could do more with Cotton. My uncle was no horseman; he was doing this just to make me happy. Throughout the ride, he made comments such as, "Boy, isn't this fun, Jean? Are you having a good time? My behind is getting a little bruised. Are we turning back soon? You think it's been an hour yet?"

I enjoyed an amazing afternoon, doing something I loved—riding a horse—with someone I loved—Uncle Glenn. After our hour-long ride, I was ecstatic and wanted to keep going. Uncle Glenn was a little worse for wear. The ride stayed with him as he hobbled around the house for the next few days.

MY UNCLES USUALLY came to visit bearing gifts from all over the world. On one of Uncle Glenn's visits, he brought home some beautiful kidskin gloves that he handpicked in France. The gloves were white, wrist length and soft as butter, very stylish. He had a half dozen pair and gave one to Mom, my sister Kaye, me and even to my friend Gayle when she was at the house. Ten minutes after Gayle left, she was back with the gloves in hand, saying her mother would not allow her to keep such a gift. My uncle was just being generous, but apparently Gayle's mother thought he might have some other motive in mind.

At times, my uncle did have ulterior motives attached to his gift giving. Years later, my sister told me a story about how he brought silk stockings home during the war when they were extremely expensive and difficult to get in the States. All silk, nylon and rayon materials were dedicated to the war effort. When Uncle Glenn went out with a woman, he gave her one stocking and told her she'd get the second one after their next date.

UNCLE GLENN LOVED TO TEASE ME, especially about Spot. He always wanted her to do tricks, and she loved to show off, so Spot gladly shook hands, played dead, spoke, sneezed, said her prayers, and howled on command. After the show, Uncle Glenn told me he was going to stick Spot in the oven. Then he paused, waiting for my reaction. I always delivered. I screamed and cried, "No, no, no," ran over and held Spot in my arms, knowing all the while he'd never do anything to hurt my dog. Uncle Glenn just sat there, grinning.

IT WAS ALWAYS A SAD DAY when Uncle Don or Uncle Glenn left. Life returned to normal. We went back to our usual routines of getting up, going to school, doing chores. The days were ordinary, not filled with surprises and the unexpected that my uncles' visits created. I hoped time passed quickly, and they'd be back with us before long.

My Neighbors

MRS. HAYES LIVED ALONE on the right side of us on Kenmore Street. She was a cranky old woman who hated *all* kids, dogs, cats and any other living creature that stepped onto her property. Old, stooped over, and wizened, Mrs. Hayes walked with a stick for support. Her house was big and dark; all the curtains remained drawn, even on pretty days, and we never saw lights in the evening. No one ever came to her home to visit.

Many days, Mrs. Hayes stood on her porch and glared at us as we played in front of our house. If we so much as stepped across the property line, she yelled at us, "Get out of my yard." Whenever Spot walked across her side yard, Mrs. Hayes picked up a rake or broom and went after her.

All of us kids *tried* to stay off her property; we really did, but the garter snakes congregated around the sidewalk of Mrs. Hayes' vacant lot. They were too tempting for Janet and me to pass up. Surprisingly, Mrs. Hayes never yelled at us when we were catching snakes. She didn't like snakes.

In the back corner of her lot were several huge clumps of pampas grass; they were at least six feet tall. We made the mistake of running through them one day and came out of the patch with huge scratches down our arms and legs. We didn't know the bushes could cut like that. For as long as we stayed in our house, we had to live next door to that grumpy old woman and her evil pampas grass.

WHEN WE FIRST MOVED to Kenmore Street in 1941, the Lindquists lived on the left side of us, on the corner. They were a nice family with two boys, Bob

A HORSE DRAWING

and Dick, both teenagers who were very mannerly. Bob had asthma and was thin; he was my favorite. He took a liking to me and sketched horse pictures for me, which I treasured.

One night, Mrs. Lindquist invited me over for dinner. She looked and sounded like the ideal mom—well spoken, always neatly dressed, nails manicured, and hair that looked like she just came from the beauty parlor. While I cleaned up, Mom ironed a pinafore sundress for me to wear; she didn't want me to embarrass her by wearing my old blue jeans with dried worms in the pockets.

I sat in the living room alone, fidgeting in my chair, while Mrs. Lindquist's two sons cleaned up for dinner. Finally, Mrs. Lindquist said dinner was ready—it smelled like roast beef—and that I should go in the bathroom and wash my hands. *Didn't she know I had taken a bath just to come to dinner?* She probably saw me digging worms earlier in the day for tomorrow's fishing trip and wanted to make doubly sure I was clean.

The Lindquists asked me questions and tried to make conversation, but it didn't amount to much. We talked some about my drawings because her son Bob was an excellent artist, but there were many uncomfortable silences when no one had anything to say. I felt as though all eyes were on me the entire night, checking to see if I had good table manners. It was difficult for me to be that well behaved for a whole night, and I was glad when the evening was over. I ran home, got out of that dress and went to help my dad roll cigarettes on his cigarette machine. He teased me about my work, saying I sometimes rolled them so tight he couldn't draw in on them.

I WAS SEVEN OR EIGHT when the Lindquists moved out, and the Bidwells moved in. Ivan and Gladys had a son named Blaine, whom they called Johnnie; I guess *Johnnie* sounded better to them than Blaine. Johnnie was stocky with blond hair and blue eyes and about my sister Linda's age. They played together a lot. He loved to tease Spot, so she stayed out of his way.

Ivan was a quiet and unassuming man. He wore bibbed overalls and stayed busy around the house, mowing the lawn and keeping the place immaculate. Gladys was a blonde, heavy set, buxom woman with a cackle you could hear a block away. She sat on her front porch glider almost every day and talked to everyone who passed by.

One night Ivan showed me how to catch night crawlers to use as fishing bait. He held onto a flashlight, and slowly, we walked through his backyard until we came up on a night crawler lying halfway out of its hole. He crept up on the worm, grabbed it and held on as it wiggled around and tried to get back into his hole. When the earthworm tired out, he pulled it out of the ground and put it in my empty vegetable can. Some of them were a foot long stretched out. Ivan caught a few more and then had me try. I broke a few of them in half, and a couple burrowed into the ground before I could grab them. He patiently stayed with me until I had enough for my fishing trip.

IVAN OWNED A PLOT OF LAND in Russell, about fifteen miles away, where he raised a garden every summer. As soon as he finished work each day, he came home, changed clothes, and drove out to the garden. Ivan knew how much I loved horses, so one day, he surprised me with an offer to go with him and ride the work horse he used to plow and rake the field for planting.

The ride to Russell seemed endless even though it took only twenty minutes. Every couple of minutes, I asked, "Are we almost there, Ivan?"

He patiently answered each time, "Any minute now, Jean, any minute now."

By the time we arrived, the old farmer was waiting for us, and he had the horse and plow ready for Ivan. The horse stood about sixteen hands high. He was a big, old brown horse with a black mane and tail, huge hooves and a broad back, and he had that delicious horsey smell I dearly loved. I patted him on his sweaty neck and rear and used my hand to shoo the flies away from his eyes.

Ivan picked me up and plopped me on the horse's back and said, "Hold on tight. I'll take the reins and steer him." For the next four hours with my legs sticking straight out at the horse's sides, I held onto the big horse's collar; I was in heaven. Both the horse and my jeans from the ankles to my backside were drenched with sweat, and I brought that horsey smell home with me. Eventually, Mom made me take off my jeans for a bath, and I lost the wonderful scent, but I was forever grateful to Ivan for that memorable day.

THE CARLSONS—Mr. and Mrs. Carlson and their daughters Lois and Janet, my sometimes friend, sometimes enemy—lived across the street from the Bidwells. An older daughter, Lavonne, lived in the basement with her two children for a while, but they kept to themselves. I never saw a husband come around. Janet never said much about Lavonne, and I didn't ask, but

JEAN, BEVERLY BUDD AND LOIS CARLSON

I thought the whole situation was kind of strange. Mr. and Mrs. Carlson's adult son Stanley and his sister Imogene and her husband visited their parents every so often. Mr. Carlson ran an automobile repair shop in the back of his house that took up half the block on West Street. Mrs. Carlson was a homemaker and a very religious woman.

To the left of the Bidwells' home was West Street and Mrs. Sisson's house. She was another cranky, old woman who hated everyone, dogs included. She rarely came out of her house, but if Spot even stepped in her yard, she shot out the door and screamed at Spot to get off her lawn. I often saw the front curtains part and a pair of eyes glaring at me. She spent most of her time looking out that window, waiting for someone to yell at. I wasn't surprised that she lived alone. I always thought she and Mrs. Hayes should room together; they could make each other miserable and leave the rest of us alone.

The Budds lived next door to Mrs. Sisson. Mr. and Mrs. Budd's daughter Beverly was my sister Kaye's good friend. Lilies of the Valley grew along the side of the Budd's house, and every spring, I picked a few of the fragrant, bell flowers and took them home to Mom. She placed them in a little vase, and their sweet smell filled our house. Lily of the Valley was one of my favorite flowers and still is.

THE BOYDS' HOME SAT next to the Budds. Susie and Daddy Boyd was an elderly couple who loved having company. Standing only four feet, ten inches tall, Susie was plump and always had a twinkle in her eye and a smile on her face. Daddy Boyd was not much taller and rotund. When he sat on the front porch steps, he looked like a big ball. The two of them spent a lot of time sitting on the porch, watching the world go by, and visiting with anyone who stopped to talk. The neighborhood children congregated at the Boyd's house to listen to them tell stories about growing up. Genuinely interested in us, they often asked about our days and what we did.

Donnie and I mowed their lawn every week for fifty cents apiece. They had a great mower with sharp blades that was easy to push. We finished the job in a jiffy, an easy fifty cents.

Susie grew beautiful red, pink and white hollyhocks on the side of their house that I used to make hollyhock dolls. When in bloom, I picked fully opened flowers and a few buds with just a bit of color showing and turned them into what looked like little dancers. I always made a few and lined them up on the front steps for Suzie to see. She loved them.

LINDA ON THE CAMPBELLS' FRONT STEPS

A YOUNG COUPLE, Mr. and Mrs. Brown, and their son Bobbie lived next to the Boyds. Bobbie's parents were quite protective of him; he was not allowed outdoors without them. Maybe they did not want him influenced by a bunch of little ragamuffins like us, so we didn't see much of him.

PHIL AND RUTH CAMPBELL occupied the house next to the Browns with Ruth's mother, whom we called Aunt Pearl. She was an elderly woman, tall and thin, and blind. Aunt Pearl taught me how to cup my hands and clap them on my knees to make the sound of a horse galloping. I loved that. Now I could add a soundtrack to my daydreams. The Campbells had a playful Airedale named Pobbie. He broke his front leg once and had it in a cast for a while. The neighborhood kids often went to visit the Campbells as they sat out on their front porch, enjoying the evening breezes.

Some years later, Ruth died suddenly of a heart attack, and Aunt Pearl took her own life shortly thereafter. I guess she felt lost without her daughter and did not want to burden her son-in-law Phil.

GARAGE AT THE BACK OF THE NEIGHBORS' HOUSES

THE BACK OF EACH of the five houses on West Street had a connected, one-car garage with a driveway between the Browns' and the Boyds' homes. Wasps liked to build nests in the rafters of these garages, which made it difficult for everyone to get in or out of their cars without getting stung. Some of the nests were six inches across. When Donnie and I couldn't find anything better to do, we grabbed a clothesline pole from the Boyds' back-yard, knocked down some of the wasps' nests, and ran like hell until they quieted down. As soon as the coast was clear, we made another pass and repeated the process until all the nests lay scattered about on the garage floors. Then, of course, we had to open up the cells and examine the contents to see what stages of development the wasps were in. We stomped the larvae with our shoes or sticks to make sure none of the wasps survived. By the time we were done, we had a pile of pulverized wasp nests and guts. The neighbors loved us for getting rid of the wasps, but they probably weren't crazy about having to clean up the mess.

THE COLVINS lived at the east end of Kenmore Street on Conewango Avenue in a big, old two-story wooden house that hadn't seen a coat of paint in twenty-five years. A large wraparound porch ran across the front and down one side of the house, making it the place where the nine Colvin children and most of the neighborhood kids congregated.

Everything about the Colvins' house was old. The inside was filled with worn out furniture, and we cooked greasy potato chips in an electric pot on a sticky dining room table. The drain pipe in the kitchen sink was broken, so they had a big tub sitting beneath the pipe to catch the dirty water. The house had its own scent—a combination of dusty, old upholstery, reused oil and rotten water. The water smelled like the pig pens at the State Hospital where we went to see the baby pigs with our Uncle Chuck.

I rarely saw Mr. and Mrs. Colvin because they worked as did a few of the older children. Tommy and Mary were our friends; Tommy was a year older than I, and Mary, a year younger. One of our favorite pastimes was playing *mushball* in the large, vacant field next to their house. Mushball was like softball but played with a larger, softer ball that didn't require the use of baseball gloves. A pick-up game of mushball pulled in kids from all over the neighborhood, and sometimes, we had as many as fifteen players. When we didn't have enough for two teams, we sat on the front porch and told stories or spent the afternoon playing hide-and-seek or kick-the-can.

After dark one evening, when we had a large group of kids at the Colvins' house, we decided to *pretend* we had a rope stretched across Conewango Avenue to stop the cars. Seven of us stood behind one another on each side of the busy road, stretched out our arms, planted our feet on the ground, leaned forward and then back as a car approached, making like we were in a tug of war with the group across the street. As soon as drivers saw us, they screeched to a halt, and we ran and hid. We did this a number of times, all with the same results, until someone called the police. We then disappeared into the night and went home, chuckling all the way at how clever we were.

The big maple trees in front of the Colvins' house provided hours of entertainment for us. On hot summer afternoons, we climbed one of the trees and sat on its big limbs, talking and watching the cars go by, just enjoying the cool shade the leaves provided. Sometimes we bought Dubble Bubble gum at Churchill's Grocery, climbed up the trees and had contests to see who could blow the biggest bubbles.

One summer when I was ten, I liked a boy named Dale who visited our neighborhood for a few weeks. He climbed up the maple tree with me, pulled out his pocketknife and carved both his and my initials with a heart around them into the trunk. He was my first crush. , but he left when summer ended. Far from brokenhearted, I returned to my dreams of trusty steeds and conquering the world.

The State Hospital Caper

IT WAS HOT AND HUMID when Donnie, Janet and I put bathing suits on under our clothes and went to the Wetmore Eddy for a dip in the *crick*, the perfect answer to a scorching July day. The walk up West Street to the eddy usually took about fifteen minutes, but anticipation of the refreshing water sped us up a bit.

Arriving at the eddy, the tall oaks cast cool shadows on the marshy ground. The water of the slow-moving *crick* sparkled, inviting us to jump in and enjoy a cool dunk. We stripped down to our bathing suits and waded into the shallows, careful to avoid the sharp rocks. We never gave any thought to the rumor that the State Hospital for the Insane in Warren, Pennsylvania had a huge drain pipe from its septic tank that emptied into the *crick* one-hundred feet upstream.

After we soaked for a while, skipped stones and looked for *crabs* (For some reason, we called *crawfish crabs;* I'm not sure why. They really were crawfish.), Donnie had what he thought was a great idea. "Why don't we wade across the *crick* and explore the tunnels at the hospital?" he asked.

"I don't know about that. Aren't there crazy people over there?" said Janet.

I looked at her wide-eyed. "Yeah, I don't want to run into any crazy people." I wasn't even sure that I knew what a crazy person looked like, but just the thought of coming face-to-face with one sent a cold chill down my back.

"C'mon you two," Donnie said. "It will be fun. We'll wade across the *crick*, climb the bank and head over to the hospital and just take a look around."

"Well, how deep is the *crick*?" I asked. I couldn't swim a lick, and both Donnie and Janet were taller than me.

"The deepest part is about up to your chest," said Donnie, putting his hand up against his thin frame, showing me where the water level would reach.

Janet never said a word.

"All right, what am I supposed to do with my clothes?" I asked.

"Hold 'em over your head, so they won't get wet. We'll put them back on after we get to the other side." Donnie always had all the answers. He was tough to argue with.

The creek was approximately seventy-five feet across. Donnie and Janet went in ahead of me. I gingerly stepped into the rock-strewn water. As the water level got higher, so did my fears. "Hey, I'm not sure this is such a great idea," I yelled out to Donnie. The water was then waist deep, and I was only one quarter of the way across.

"Oh come on," Donnie said. "Don't be such a baby."

Donnie knew calling me a baby would keep me going. Donnie and I were extremely competitive, and there was no way I was going to let him have anything on me. *Okay, I can do this; yes I can.* Deeper, deeper—the water crept up to my chest. Halfway there. With the water up to my chin, I spotted a brown clump of *something* floating by me. "What is that brown glob that just went by me, Donnie?"

He glanced back to see what I was talking about. "Oh, that's just a little poop, Jean. Forget about it."

"*Ick!* This is disgusting." *Oh my God, I'm going to die from poop if I don't drown first.* The water came up to my nose with my next few steps, so I threw back my head and hopped up and down, hoping it wouldn't get any deeper. Thank God, it didn't; the creek got shallower from that point on. I decided I was going to live, though I knew I'd end up with some dreaded disease from the dirty water.

Once on the other side, we climbed the steep, slippery bank, muddying up our hands and knees in the process. Our clothes stuck to our wet bodies as we quickly pulled on our tee shirts and shorts. To reach our destination, we had to walk through a lush, green field owned by the hospital, cross the highway and sneak onto the grounds.

"C'mon, this way," said Donnie. He apparently had been here before and knew the way. Janet and I didn't have any idea of where we were headed, so we blindly followed Donnie. "We have to get to the tunnels before anyone sees us."

"What are these tunnels anyway?" I asked. "The deep water was bad enough. I don't want to go walking through some dark tunnel."

"No it's nothing like that," Donnie said. "You'll see." I later found out that these tunnels were designed for ventilation. When the hospital was built back in 1874, huge fans pulled air through these tunnels creating a natural form of air conditioning that vented fresh air into every room.

Janet and I followed closely behind Donnie until we reached an opening among the huge buildings. "You know," I said, "I heard they cut peoples' heads open and take out their brains here if they're bad. Is that true, Donnie?"

"Yeah, and they have this machine they use to give them bad shocks to wake them up," he said.

Janet piped up as we approached the tunnel entrance, "We might see one of them. If we do, they'll probably catch us and take us somewhere in the tunnels, tie us up and shock us. Then we'll *never* see our families again." She turned around quickly and grabbed my arm. I screamed.

"*Shhh*, Jean" Donnie said. "You're going to get us in trouble." With all this talk, the entrance to the tunnel just ahead seemed darker and more sinister than I imagined.

"Are you scared, Jeannie?" asked Janet.

"Maybe...a little." I wrapped my arms around my body to ward off the unnatural chill I felt and to protect myself from what might be lurking in that tunnel.

It took a minute for my eyes to get used to the dimness in the passageway, but when they did, I saw that the arched walls and floors were made of rough bricks. I had to watch closely where I stepped to keep from tripping. The tunnel was about eight-feet wide and seven-feet tall and filled with a musty odor. The twisting corridors went on forever. From somewhere in the distance, I heard the steady hum of fans and felt the whoosh of stale air moving through the passageways.

Donnie was right; this was a great place even though it was a bit spooky. Just then a shadowy figure rumbled by us with a cart of what looked like food trays. He passed right next to us and acted like he did not even see us. *Was this one of the crazy people?* I felt another cold shiver run down my spine.

"Hey, look at this," Donnie said, pointing out the row of doors running the entire length of the tunnel, all closed. Curiosity got the best of us, and we swung open the first door and flicked on the light. Bathroom fixtures. The entire room was filled with old toilets, sinks, bathtubs and pipes. *Boring.* The next door opened to a room full of furniture—bedside tables, metal bed frames, dining room chairs stacked every which way, upended tables, legs pointing to the sky. *Better, but not very exciting.* We found everything needed for a hundred kitchens—pots, pans, dishes, forks, spoons—behind the third door, but it wasn't until we opened the fourth door that we found something really exciting. *Mattresses...* a room full of used mattresses piled up close to the ceiling, allowing just enough of a gap for us to become airborne and not hit our heads. Donnie, Janet and I looked at each other; huge grins spread across our faces. We couldn't resist. We closed the door behind us and launched into some serious jumping.

"I can jump higher than you," I shouted.

"Yeah right, you little snot, look at this," Donnie said as he did a flip, landing on his back.

"Big deal, look how many somersaults I can do," I yelled back.

Janet stopped for a second, scrunched up her nose and said, "It kind of stinks in here. And what are all the spots on these mattresses?"

"I dunno," Donnie said. "Just jump around them." We hadn't given one thought to the previous lives of these *used* mattresses and what remnants of those earlier existences remained deep in the padding. We jumped, tumbled and bounced for at least an hour, until we were all hot, sweaty and dirty.

At the point of exhaustion, Donnie decided that we should leave the hospital and head for home as it was late in the afternoon. We slowly cracked open the mattress-room door and looked up and down the tunnel to see if the coast was clear, afraid that maybe someone heard us yelling and laughing and was waiting to haul us off to that dark and scary room. We didn't see anyone, so we hurried out of the tunnel into the bright sunlight. When we got to the road we had previously crossed, Donnie thought we should hitchhike home, so we didn't have to wade across the creek again. That was fine by me. I might not have been so lucky the second time. I might have fallen in a hole and drowned, never to be seen again.

We had seen people hitchhiking before, so we knew what to do. Standing on the side of the road, we put our thumbs out and waited. It wasn't long before a car with an older couple—they must have been all of thirty, but to our young eyes, they were old—passed by us slowly and pulled over to the side of the road. The woman rolled down the window asked if we needed a ride. We all yelled, "Sure," and jumped into the back seat.

"What are your names, and where do you live?" the man asked in a soft voice. He was dressed in a suit and tie.

Donnie spoke for us, telling him our names and that we lived in Hooktown (a section of Warren) on Kenmore Street. "But you can drop us off on the corner of Conewango and Kenmore," Donnie said. "We can walk from there." Donnie was smart; he didn't want our parents to see us getting out of a strange car.

During the fifteen-minute ride home, the lady did most of the talking, asking us all kinds of questions—what were our parents' names, how old were we, did we have brothers and sisters. She had beautiful, red curly hair and green-green eyes that fascinated me when she looked over the front seat to talk with us. She wore a nice dress and a small hat. She and the man looked like they were going to a dinner party. We thanked the couple as they pulled up to the curb near our street. Janet went across the road to her house, and we walked up the driveway to ours.

Mom was in the kitchen starting dinner when we strolled into the house. "Hi kids, where have you been all day?" she asked.

"We went swimming in the *crick*. We're all dirty, so we're going to take a bath, okay?" Donnie explained. Wednesdays and Saturdays were our usual bath nights, but whenever we were overly sweaty or dirty, we took a bath, regardless of what day it was. I cleaned up first, put on fresh clothes and

MY DRAWING OF WILDFIRE

went downstairs to wait for dinner while Donnie took his bath. The news played on the radio in the living room while I sat on the floor, drawing a new version of Wildfire, the magnificent red stallion in the Zane Grey westerns. I *loved* horses, and I drew them all the time. This one was fiery like the horses that lived in my nightly dreams. They had long flowing manes and tails and arched muscular necks, proud horses, prancing around the field of my imagination, pawing the ground, but my horses were always well-trained and manageable.

When Daddy came home from his job at the post office, he went into the kitchen and talked to Mom in a low voice; I couldn't make out what he was saying. I figured they were just discussing some boring adult stuff, so I went back to my drawing.

When Donnie made his way down the stairs, Dad said, "Hey kids, come here for a second. I want to ask you something." From the tone of his voice, I could tell something was up. Plus, he didn't usually call us to him right after he got home; he liked to spend the time before dinner catching up with Mom. After we walked into the kitchen, Dad looked straight at us, "Where did you go today?"

Again Donnie spoke for us, "Oh, we went swimming up at the Wetmore Eddy and then came right home." If there was any lying to be done, Donnie had to do it. Any time I was asked something directly, I always spilled my guts.

"Well, that's interesting," Daddy replied. "I was just talking to a couple I know, and they said you two were hitchhiking in North Warren. They picked you up and brought you home. Is that right?"

Donnie and I looked at each other and then fixed our eyes on the linoleum floor. We were caught, yet again. Our great, adventurous day ended bleakly right there in the kitchen. Daddy warmed our bottoms good that night, forbade us to ever go to the hospital or hitchhike again, and grounded us for the next three days. For the next three days, all of our escapades would have to take place within the confines of our house and backyard. *Jeeez.*

Grounded

WHAT COULD DONNIE and I do since we were grounded and confined to our house and yard for three days? Our hitchhiking incident landed us in this predicament. We had to find a way to entertain ourselves without leaving our property. Friends were off limits as well, so we were stuck with each other and our imaginations.

As we sat at the kitchen table the next morning, eating our breakfast of hot cocoa and toast slathered with butter—a whole loaf's worth—we decided we needed a place of our own where we could play and not be bothered by adults. Our plan was launched. Donnie and I would dig a secret room for us to play in, and we knew the perfect spot for it—behind the garage. We wolfed down the remainder of our breakfast and ran out the door to survey the area and make a plan.

WE HAD A LARGE BACKYARD bordered by five-foot hedges on all sides. Each year, Daddy had part of the area plowed for a small garden by an old farmer and his horse. There he and Mom planted potatoes, corn, green beans, tomatoes, radishes and lettuce that we ate all summer long. The only way my parents could get me to do chores I didn't want to do was to pay me; weeding the garden was one of those dreaded tasks. I got paid a quarter a row to pull weeds, so I did it even though I hated the job. The back of this space was always saved for the most beautiful varieties of flowers—zinnias, marigolds and dahlias—that Mom cut and placed in vases throughout our house in spring and summer.

In the back left-hand corner of the yard was the ugliest tree I ever saw. Looking like an ancient, stooped-over, old man who was rotting away limb by limb and just wouldn't die, this wormy tree grew the sourest green apples ever. Just the thought of chomping into one of those hard, misshapen apples made my jaws hurt, plus there was always a good chance of biting a worm in half. *Eeeeeooooouuuu.* Picturing that made me want to throw up.

The tree had to be at least thirty years old. Dad kept it, because it provided some privacy, so we didn't have to look at the neighbor's home. But if anyone stared at their house, they'd see two of Donnie's arrows stuck into the second floor wall. Donnie was aiming at the apple tree and missed his mark. Whenever we wanted an apple, we went right past that old tree over to the Samuelson's yard to pick the Macintosh and the Red and Yellow Delicious apples off the ground.

The several Japanese plum trees we had more than made up for the sour apples. The plums were small—the size of the ball I used to play jacks with—but they were sweet and juicy. Before I ate one, I rubbed its smooth, dark skin on my clothes to get off its powder-like coating and made it shiny, almost blue-black. It tasted better to me that way.

Peony bushes with big pink, red and white blooms lined the right side of the yard. I liked the red ones best. I loved to watch ants crawl over the peony buds and help the flowers open by eating away some of the thick, waxy stuff on the bud. Along with the sweet scent of the peonies, fragrant lavender and white lilac bushes grew on the side of our yard. At times Mom cut some lilacs off the bush and brought them into the house. Then a sweet, fresh smell filled the rooms.

The kid-and-dog-hating Mrs. Hayes lived on the other side of the lilac bushes. The smell of the lilacs didn't sweeten up her personality, that's for sure. I knew she was a witch, a real one. I pictured her flying out of the second floor window on a broom, swooping down and putting a hex on us. Often I had nightmares of Mrs. Hayes chasing me and holding me prisoner in a dark room upstairs. In the dream, I'd see myself looking out her window toward our house, but no one could see or hear me. That nightmare scared me awake every time. I always kept a wary eye on Mrs. Hayes and that house next door when I was outside. I had to watch closely because she was so short; I could only see the top of her head above the hedges.

ALONGSIDE THE GARAGE, the fresh smell of mint filled the air, and the tall, red stalks of rhubarb guarded the structure. Every summer, Mom made rhubarb pies and rhubarb sauce we poured into a small dish and ate with a spoon. The sauce was tart and made my mouth pucker up, so a little bit went a long way. It was so sour, it even hurt my jaws. Sometimes Donnie and I broke off shoots, peeled off the red skin and sprinkled salt on the crunchy, whitish-yellow stalks. The salt took away the tartness.

It was there, in the midst of all the beauty and sweet smells that my brother and I decided to build our haven. "How big should we make it, Donnie?" I asked.

"Well, let me think," he answered. I could tell he was thinking; he always squinted his eyes when he was deep in thought. He walked off a big square, setting his heels down at each corner to mark the territory for digging. "Ok, let's get the tools from the garage and start in." We pulled out everything we might need—a shovel, spade, hoe and rake—anything to make the digging easier.

I got a vegetable can out of the garbage and put some dirt in it for the worms we dug up. I always needed worms for fishing. As we turned over each shovelful, I reminded Donnie to look out for any nightcrawlers or grubs, those little, fat, white worms with black heads and pincers. The fish loved them, but I had to be careful handling them, so I didn't get pinched.

Dirt flew everywhere as our enthusiasm increased about creating this special room just for us. No adults allowed. "So, Donnie, what are you going to have in your part of the room," I asked.

"Well, I want a place to sit and read my Superman and Dick Tracy comic books," he said. "And you know, I won't run out of them any time soon, because Jack Timmis has a whole cellar full of comic books I can borrow."

"I can bring down my Nancy Drew books and maybe some of your Hardy Boys' paperbacks, if you don't mind," I said. I kept digging, but every shovelful caused my mind to wander off. *I wonder how far I have to dig to get to China. When I get close to it, am I just going to fall down into it? Once I'm there, will there be blue skies? Where would the sky come from? And when I'm ready to come home, how do I get back into the hole?*

We were hot, dirty and tired, but Donnie and I didn't want to stop for too long for lunch. Mom was making ground bologna, my favorite, so I certainly wasn't about to pass that up. She took a ring of bologna and minced it in her grinder then added in mayonnaise and relish. She made us each a sandwich and poured two glasses of milk. It was a fine lunch, but duty called. As we rushed off to continue our project, Mom gave Donnie and me a sideways glance like she knew what we were doing, but it was keeping us occupied and out of her hair, so she let us be. We still had much work to do before the day ended.

After a full day of digging, we only got down about two feet. At first it was easy, but then we hit clay, and we slowed down to a crawl. All this digging and thinking made me hungry. "Donnie, I'm getting hungry," I said. "It must be almost dinnertime, and I'm tired. We can finish tomorrow, okay?" Donnie agreed, and we went inside to get cleaned up for dinner.

Daddy came home not long after we quit for the day, and we couldn't wait to show him the work we did. Big mistake. He surveyed the beginnings of our secret room for several minutes, walked all around it slowly, and saw how carefully we had piled up the dirt all around the hole to make walls, leaving an open space for a doorway. Then he frowned at us. "We can't have this dirty mess here in the backyard. Next time it rains, this will be a mud hole," he said. "Tomorrow I want you two to fill this hole back up." Then he turned and walked back into the house.

Donnie and I looked at each other in disbelief. Tears formed at the corners of my eyes, but I didn't dare cry. That would have made me a baby. All of our hard work for nothing. Tomorrow we'd have to cover our beautiful room and forget any dreams of having our own secret place. I realized I'd probably never get to China either.

Churchill's Grocery

I SPENT A LOT OF TIME running back and forth to Churchill's Grocery for my mother when she needed bread, milk, butter, or soup, the small stuff. For our big, weekly shopping trips, my parents usually took a bus or cab to the A&P in downtown Warren. Mom always sent me to Churchill's because these trips got me out of her hair for a few minutes, and I ran faster than anyone else in the house. With each run, I tried to break my previous record.

Mom gave me the *ready-set-go* send off and began watching the time while I shot out the back door, squeezed through a hole in the hedge, raced across the Bidwells' backyard, flew down West Street past the Samuelsons' house, took a sharp right on Wilson Street, blew by where Maejean Edmiston and the Donaheys lived and dashed past an open field. Once I caught sight of the old, two-story, tan-bricked building that used to be a filling station, I pushed even harder. I sprinted across Wilson Street, jumped up the three steps and slammed the squeaky screen door behind me.

Whew! Just inside the door, I tried to catch my breath, but on a summer's day, the air inside was just as hot as it was outside. The small fan, which the Churchill's sat up on a high shelf, blew full force all day long but did little to cool the place off even though the store wasn't very big. It had only one small aisle of canned goods, bread and a candy counter on the far side with a meat counter with hamburger, roasts and steaks at the back of the store. A sheet of sticky flypaper covered with dead flies hung from the ceiling, just waiting for more victims.

I routinely ran the block or so to Churchill's in less than two minutes one

GAYLE AND SHERRY

way. My record was a minute and a half. The only thing that jeopardized a new record was the people in line ahead of me. When that happened, I stood around, shifted my weight, drummed my fingers on the countertop, and tried to hurry along the pokey customers. Mr. Samuelson never got the message; he stood at the meat counter in his dirty bib overalls with an open fly, chattering on and saying nothing. All the while, the clock kept ticking. *Didn't he know he was jeopardizing my new world record?*

A man named Winston Churchill—no relation—owned the store with his wife. It was located on Conewango Avenue, just one street over from our house and convenient for everyone in the neighborhood when they realized they were missing some ingredient and needed it right away. My friend Gayle lived just a few houses down from Churchill's Store and often ran to the store for one slice of bologna to make her school lunch. The Churchills also allowed people to charge their groceries and pay one bill at the end of the month.

Mr. and Mrs. Churchill had no children of their own but had been raising their niece, Sherry Smith, after her mother had a nervous breakdown and went to a mental hospital and never returned.

Mr. Churchill had his own problems. People said he was gassed in World War I and was never the same after that. He walked around the store, talking to himself, staring vacantly into space. He never combed his messy, gray hair, didn't tuck in his shirttails and usually had one shoe untied.

Sometimes he said things that made me uncomfortable, like the one day when he came out of the store and watched us chewing our gum and seeing who could blow the biggest bubbles. "I know when you girls will turn into women," he said. "First will be Janet, then Gayle, then Jean and last will be Sherry." As it turned out, he was accurate. At other times, Mr. Churchill asked a question and then walked off before I could answer. He always had this wild look in his eyes.

Mrs. Churchill did most of the work in the store while her husband puttered around. She was Polish and not out-going but was always nice to me. She kept her straight, black hair short, and all the work she did made her slim. Even I could tell she was tired with those dark circles under her eyes and drooping shoulders.

THE CHURCHILLS' NIECE Sherry was my age, so we palled around together when she wasn't slicing meat or working the cash register in the store or taking violin lessons. I liked Sherry. She had a pretty face with blue eyes, a turned-up nose, full cheeks and a beautiful smile. Her curly light brown hair made her look like Shirley Temple, and she was always cheerful and funny.

ONE DAY WHEN we were playing, Sherry asked, "Jeannie, do you want to get a suntan?"

"Sure. How are we going to do that?"

"We have a lamp that you can get under, and it makes you tan," Sherry said, as we climbed the back stairs to the second-floor apartment where they all lived. "It's really powerful, so we have to be real careful and not stay under it too long, or it'll burn us, bad."

We brought the lamp into Sherry's bedroom where we wouldn't be disturbed, took off our shorts and rolled up our T-shirts to maximize the tanning area. We each took a turn, lying in the bright light of the lamp, then another and another. Sweat pooled in my belly button from the heat of the bulb, but I wasn't seeing any difference in my skin.

"Are you sure about this, Sherry? I can't see any tan, and I've been under here for ten minutes," I said. "All I'm doing is sweating. That little fan isn't helping at all."

"It takes a while before you get red, Jeannie," Sherry said. "You can do your other side when I'm done."

After my fourth time under the lamp with no change in the color of my skin, I got curious and wanted to know why I wasn't tanning. I looked at the bulb, and right there in small letters, it said: *heat lamp for aching muscles*.

"Sherry, look at this. It says *heat lamp!* This isn't a sunlamp at all. Geez, what a waste of time. I'm going home; see you tomorrow."

Sherry just smiled and shrugged her shoulders. Then she flipped over and warmed her other side.

Wild Ride on the Crick

IAWOKE TO THE SOUND of April rains beating on the roof of our house. I stretched, rolled onto my back and thought about how to occupy myself indoors, since the rain didn't seem like it was going to let up any time soon. Other than the tapping of the rain drops, the house was quiet. It was Saturday morning, and no one was up yet.

Pulling on my robe, I tiptoed downstairs to let Spot out. She sat at the bottom of the stairs, as she did every morning, patiently waiting for me. I opened the front door for her. She stuck her nose out and looked back at me as if to say, *Are you crazy? It's pouring cats and dogs out there!* I prodded her with my foot, and she begrudgingly went out with both her head and tail down, knowing she was going to get soaked. She came back in a jiffy and shook herself head to toe to get rid of the water. "Stop it, Spot. You're getting me all wet."

We went into the kitchen and looked for something for breakfast. I settled on a bowl of shredded wheat and milk. It wasn't long before everyone in the house was up, and the usual Saturday chores began. In my room, I made my bed and picked up my books and drawings and put my dirty clothes in the basket in my parents' closet, but before I made it downstairs to dust the gate-legged table, the oak dining table, chairs, and highboy, I got sidetracked looking at my horse scrapbook. The scrapbook was filled with hundreds of horse photographs I cut out from magazines. I flipped through the pages displaying Man o' War, the successful thoroughbred racehorse; Whirlaway, the triple-crown winner in 1941; Dice, the black and white pinto in the movie, *Duel in the Sun*; and other show horses, including quarter horses and Arabians, my favorite breed, with their beautiful heads and bodies. I had spent hours accumulating all these photographs over the years, and I enjoyed looking through them again and again. My scrapbook also contained sketches of horses I drew. After scanning a few pages, I drifted off, daydreaming about the horse I vowed to have one day. He'd be a magnificent black or white steed, spirited but under control, a big, well-muscled horse.

WITH CHORES BEHIND US, Donnie and I decided to have a *puzzle duel*. We each picked a jigsaw puzzle—mine was of wildflowers and Donnie chose a country scene—and sat opposite each other on the dining room floor with the pieces spread out in front of us. The first one to finish the puzzle won. I had almost completed mine when I ran out of pieces, and I still had a hole in the middle. I glared at Donnie, as he yelled, "I won! I won!"

"Yeah, sure. You stole my last two pieces, you creep," I said. "Mom, Donnie stole my puzzle pieces. He cheated!"

"Quit fighting, or I'll make both of you stay in your rooms," Mom said. I gave Donnie a dirty look and went into the kitchen to make a peanut butter and jelly sandwich for lunch and poured myself a large glass of cold milk.

After lunch, the rain stopped, but the clouds were low and gray. They looked heavy. Donnie, Spot and I looked around outside for something to do and decided to walk to the crick and see how high the water was. It had been raining the last few days, so we knew the water level would be up. We put on our shin-high rubber boots, and after hooking a leash onto Spot, off we went.

We went to the *crick* by way of the Samuelsons' backyard, down their long, dirt driveway to the path behind the chicken coop. Donnie and I stopped for a minute to scoop handfuls of cracked corn to feed the hens. It fascinated me to see those chickens scurrying about, pecking up the bits of corn with satisfied clucks. We followed the path down the hill to within fifty feet of the *crick's* edge. The dark, muddy water had risen about a foot or so, and the current ran much quicker than usual because of all the rain.

"Let's go down to the bank and see what we can find to do," Donnie said. We walked down the hill to the water's edge and made a new path alongside the *crick* because the rising water had covered the old trail. Three hundred or so feet down, we came across something too good to be true.

"Hey, look, someone left a boat tied up to a tree," I said. "I wonder who it belongs to. The oars are here, too." We examined the boat, and it looked safe and sturdy.

"I know what we can do," Donnie said. "We can take the boat across the *crick* and go see the Andersons."

"That's a great idea, but what am I going to do with Spot?"

"Bring her. Tie her leash to the seat, so she won't jump out," Donnie offered as a solution.

We found a can and took turns bailing the water out of the boat. I tied Spot to the seat in the front, and I sat in the middle. Donnie untied and pushed off the boat from the bank. As soon as he jumped in, we grabbed the oars, but the boat's bow immediately turned downstream and got caught in the fast-moving water. No matter how hard we tried to get the boat into the middle of the *crick*, we could not change its direction.

"Row, Jean, row!" Donnie screamed. "The current is carrying us downstream." Waves pounded the sides of the boat, filling it with water. We screamed directions at each other, but no matter what we tried, the boat raced down the *crick* at an alarming speed.

By now, the boat was twenty feet from shore and not responding to anything we did. The Conewango Dam was only a mile away, and at the rate we were moving, we were going to reach the dam in no time. There we'd surely be turned over and pulled underwater, never to be seen again.

"Jump, Jean!" Donnie yelled. We both let go of the oars and plunged into the freezing, spring water. Thankfully, the water was only hip deep at this point, so we were able to stand up and wade toward shore. Then I realized Spot was still in the boat, tied to the front seat. She looked at me for reassurance that everything was going to be all right. I stood there, frozen, screaming at her to stay in the boat. Terrible images of her drowning or being strangled by the leash raced through my mind.

I caught a glimpse of a man in a bright yellow raincoat and waders, carrying a fishing pole. He waded into the water downstream, reached out his arm, grabbed ahold of the boat and hauled it to the bank. I ran to where he was and untied Spot as I cried and thanked the man over and over for saving my dog. I held Spot in my arms, and she covered my face with kisses.

The man was kind but sternly told us how lucky we were to be alive and that we should never take anyone else's boat without permission. "Now, go home and get dry. You're shivering," he said. "Think about what I just said, and remember to thank God that you're okay."

After we promised we'd never do a foolish thing like this again, we went our separate ways. I felt thankful that we didn't get hurt, but most of all, I was so grateful to have my little dog back.

DONNIE AND I WALKED HOME slowly, knowing we were in big trouble. Two soaked children and one wet dog—evidence of our guilt. We opened the side door and stepped into the house not knowing what to expect from Mom. She stared at us and finally asked, "What in the world happened to you two?"

Donnie paused slightly and then poured out his story. "Well, Jean and I went down to the crick. Spot saw something on the other side and raced into the water after it," Donnie said. "We both jumped into the water to save her. That's how we all got so wet."

Man, if she believes this one, she'll believe anything, I thought to myself. I wasn't going to outright lie about our situation, but if she accepted Donnie's version, so much the better. Mom told us to put Spot in the basement, go upstairs and take a nice, warm bath and then come down to dinner.

When Daddy came home from work, Mom told him the story, and we had a nice, quiet evening, listening to *Amos 'n' Andy* and *Your Hit Parade* on the radio. The next morning, Donnie and I walked to church and stopped in at Adam's Grocery Store to spend our Sunday School money on candy, as we usually did. We went to school on Monday, and the scary scene at the *crick* was a thing of the past.

ON MONDAY EVENING, Daddy came home at the usual time and sat in the living room, reading the *Warren Times Mirror* newspaper. "Pearl," he called out to my mom in the kitchen, "come in here and read this article. Donnie and Jean, you might like to hear this, too." Donnie and I looked at each other but didn't say a word.

"This article talks about how a fisherman saved a little girl and boy and their dog from drowning in the creek last Saturday," Daddy said. "Could that have been you two?" Donnie and I kept our heads down as we received another lecture about what a dangerous thing we did and how we should never take another person's property without permission. What they were most upset about, though, was that Donnie lied about the whole mess. I thought sure a serious punishment would follow, but it didn't. My parents must have been grateful we were not harmed.

I learned some valuable lessons that Saturday afternoon, especially to stay away from the water when it gets high and never to jeopardize my dog's life by tying her up in a boat. I hugged Spot that much tighter every time I thought of how I easily could have lost her forever.

A Summer Day's Fun

THE JULY SUN beat down on us as Donnie, Janet and I sat on the front porch steps, deciding how we'd spend one of the last days before school began. What could we do? Mom had already warned us to stay out of the road and not to play in the oil after the city sprayed Kenmore Street. Maintenance workers routinely applied oil to unpaved roads to keep the dust down, and our street was to be treated that day.

While trying to figure out what to do, we noticed the ice truck coming down the road. Only one house on our street still had an icebox rather than an electric refrigerator, so each week, the iceman delivered just one block. The truck was a ramshackle old thing with a tarp canopy pulled down over the blocks of ice to keep them from melting. As soon as he grabbed the block with heavy tongs and carried it to the back of the house, we jumped up, ran to the truck and looked for broken pieces of ice to suck on. We brought our finds back to the steps and enjoyed this cool treat as the melting ice dripped down our arms and into our laps. We sucked on those ice chips until they were gone.

WE RELAXED ON THE STEPS, waiting for the oil truck. We knew what we were planning, but no one said it aloud. When the truck finally arrived, we watched as thick, hot oil sprayed out of holes in a long pipe attached to a tank at the back of the truck. The vapor from the hot oil floated into the air. When we could no longer see any signs of heat, Donnie whispered, "Okay, Jean, I think it's cool enough now." We needed to be quiet because Mom had the front door open and could hear us if she tried. We got up and slowly walked to the road.

Tiny rivulets of oil wended their way from the middle to the sides of the road and created little pools before being absorbed by the dirt.

Donnie stuck his bare toe into a glob of oil first to check the temperature. "Ouch, that's still hot. Let's get some twigs until it cools off." We scurried around the front yard, looking for sticks. We used them to stir the goop, make designs with it until Janet got a little too enthusiastic and flung oil onto my legs.

"Yuk, Janet," I said. "How am I going to get this off now?" I gathered a bunch of leaves in the front yard and tried to wipe away the oil. That didn't work. Now a mixture of oil and dirt covered my legs. By the time we finished, we were all covered in oil. I sneaked down to the cellar and took a bar of the yellow Fels-Naptha soap Mom used to get stains out of our clothes. We cleaned up as best we could, using the soap at the water spigot at the side of the house.

Janet went home for lunch, and Donnie and I crept into the kitchen to fix peanut butter and strawberry jam sandwiches and pour glasses of milk. We got the job done but had almost as much peanut butter and jelly on the counter as we did on the slices of white bread. Mom called to us from upstairs, "What's going on down there? Do I smell oil?"

"Nah, Mom, we're just making our lunch," I said. Donnie and I quickly wiped down the counter with the dishcloth, grabbed our sandwiches and milk and ran out the back door before Mom could make it down the stairs. I loved to eat on the patio at the picnic table in the backyard. It was an 8' x 10' area right behind the garage that Daddy dug out, leveled with sand and covered with bricks. After Donnie and I dug a large hole in that spot to build our own rooms, Daddy figured he'd best do something with the area before we tried to destroy the yard once again. Sitting out there, I could smell the flowers, listen to the wrens and robins chirp and feel the soft, summer breezes on my sweaty skin.

Janet came back over after lunch, and we decided to put on our swimsuits and go down to the *crick* behind the Samuelson's house for a swim. Sometimes we went inside Mr. Samuelson's barn just to look around. On the walls made of rough, unpainted boards, someone had glued pictures cut from old magazines. One entire side and part of the back were covered in pictures of movie stars, horses, dogs, cars, advertisements, cowboys and just about anything one could imagine. We often spent a half hour or more, staring at the photos and trying to figure out whom they might be, but not today. We were ready to take a dip in the *crick*.

We always stuck a foot into the water first to see how cold it was, but this July it was like warm bath water. The water level was low, so we waded

JEAN, DONNIE AND KAYE — SUMMER 1945

out until only our heads stuck out above the surface. We dodged sticks and blobs—the origin of which I did not want to know—and kept moving, so the bloodsuckers didn't latch onto us. I was learning how to swim, so I practiced kicking, the breaststroke and the dog paddle. Other times, we held hands and bobbed up and down. If we were lucky, we had an inner tube to use as a float. Spot, as always, was right there with us. She searched up and down the bank for something to chase and finally gave up, lay down in the grass and dozed off.

Every year when the summer began, I felt like I had forever to play and do as I pleased. On that hot summer day at the *crick*, I knew my independence was coming to an end; lessons and homework lurked right around the corner. My time would soon no longer be my own. School was okay, but I liked the freedom and ease of a summer day so much more.

Elusive Dream: Search for Horses

THE BAD PEOPLE CLOSED IN, and my beautiful steed tired. His sides heaved, and flecks of foam flew from his mouth. I hunched over Windstar's back; his wavy, black mane whipped my face. I spurred him on, over the mountains into the thick forest. There we could hide. One of the outlaws, now right on top of us, reached across to grab me...

I snapped awake, soaked in a cold sweat with my pajamas sticking to my body, the blankets thrown aside in my attempts to outride these criminals. Thank God. I was at home in my bed, listening to the soft breaths of my sleeping sisters, Kaye and Linda. They slept soundly, oblivious to my plight. *Tonight, before I go to bed, I will definitely rewrite the ending of that dream.*

While my heart rate returned to normal, I listened to the early morning sounds outside our bedroom window—the steady beat of droplets from the fog hitting the porch roof, leaves from the maple tree brushing back and forth against the eaves of our house, and the cooing of a nearby pigeon. The fall dampness crept into our room through the open window, sending a shiver up my spine.

Just then, I remembered it was Saturday, and I was wasting time when there was a whole world outside that window that needed to be explored. I grabbed my clothes, dressed in the warm bathroom and headed downstairs to Spot's welcoming kisses. By the time I walked her and raced through my Saturday chores, the sun had broken through the fog. *Time to go.* I jumped on Kaye's bike, and Spot ran alongside me.

I SAILED UP KENMORE STREET to the corner and stopped to check both ways for cars before crossing. No cars but I caught sight of a mound of steaming *something* on the other side of the road. I walked my bike over and looked down on a big pile of smelly, but fascinating, horse poop. After considerable study and thought, I came to the conclusion that if there was poop, there had to be a horse, and by the size of this heap, I knew this was no pony. Vapor rose from the still-warm droppings, so the horse must be close by. The hoof marks in the mound told me there were multiple horses, and they were heading north on Conewango Avenue.

I put Spot in the basket on the front of the bike and sped off—up Conewango past Willoughy Avenue beyond Quaker Hill and the Old Ladies Home past more poop and then by the Conewango Dam. Coming around a bend in the road, I spotted them in the distance, clip-clopping up the paved road. I stood on the pedals and caught up to them quickly, and then hung back and admired the horses from the rear. I didn't want to get too close for fear that someone would tell me to go home. I inhaled deeply, taking in that wonderful horse smell coming off the troop just ahead.

On an excursion into the country, the riders turned the horses onto Hatch Run Road where Gardeners Rocks was. Hikers and rock climbers loved Gardeners Rocks because it had massive boulders and tree roots growing in and out of the outcropping. I never went there. I heard too many stories about poisonous copperhead snakes that lived in those rocks.

I felt relieved when the riders passed the dirt road leading to the rocks and dismounted just up the road at a small pavilion to eat their picnic lunches. I parked my bike and stood close by, admiring the horses. They were just regular animals—bays, duns and a couple of quarter horses—but I thought *every* horse was magnificent. I lurked around, desperately wishing someone would ask me if I wanted to sit on one of their horses. One female rider who wore jodhpurs and English boots noticed me and asked where I lived. When I told her, she said, "You are a long way from home, little girl. Do you want to pet my horse?" I jumped at the chance. Stroking this beautiful animal and getting that wonderful horse smell all over me more than compensated for the two-mile bike ride.

Spot had no interest in the horses; she was off tracking squirrels, rabbits and any other critter that ran when chased. After a time, I put Spot back in the basket and reluctantly headed toward home. I stopped at Churchill's Grocery on the way and bought some Dubble Bubble gum and a coke for me and got Mom her beloved Heath Bar as a surprise with the fifty cents Dad paid me to shine his shoes.

I spent the rest of the afternoon at home with pens and paper, sketching the horses I saw earlier, daydreaming about the day I would have one of my own. Later I worked on a scenario for that night's dream where I could ride my graceful and spirited Friesian, save the women and children, catch the villains, and ride into town a hero.

Muddy Pond

HEY, JEAN, WHAT YOU DOING?" I recognized Gayle's voice on the other end of the phone.

"Nothin' right now, just ate breakfast," I answered. "Why?"

"Mom doesn't have anything for me to do, so let's go to the prairie and play horses. Bring a lunch. We can spend the day out there."

Playing horses at the prairie—what we called the old fairgrounds—sounded like a great idea to me. I loved to go to the woods, especially since I never knew what kind of varmint we might run into. When we played horses, we gave ourselves names and pretended to be horses in pursuit by the bad guys. Evil ranchers wanted to capture and tame us because we were free and fearless. We protected our herd of mares and made sure no harm came to them or us. We raced across the prairie and through the woods, whinnying and kicking our way to safety. It was one of our favorite games.

I told my mom where I was going, made my old standby lunch, a peanut butter and jelly sandwich, and ran out the door with Spot. On the way to Gayle's, I stopped at Churchill's Grocery for a bottle of root beer. Gayle jumped up from her front porch and fell into step with me as we walked up the street to Quaker Hill Road, behind the old ladies' home, as we called Watson Memorial Home, to the stream next to the prairie. We splashed around a bit in the cool water and turned over rocks, looking for salamanders and crawfish, and eventually made it to the path on the other bank. Just off the trail, I spotted a large gray snake. It was coiled up, sunning itself on a flat boulder next to a second stream. Its thick body and triangular head told me it was probably poisonous, so we gave it a wide berth.

A few minutes later, Gayle and I found a shady spot for our lunches and marked out the territory for playing horses. We pretended to be a different horse every time. "I'm Wildfire today, Gayle." Wildfire was my shiny red stallion with his long, flowing black mane and tail and my favorite pretend-horse. "Who are you?"

"Oh, I'll be Silver Cloud."

"Good," I said. "Now the bad guys are after us, so we have to kick 'em and then run as fast as we can to get away. Got it?" With that said, Gayle bucked and kicked and ran onto the prairie with me right behind her. When we couldn't run anymore, we plopped down on the ground and rested until we had enough energy to walk back to where we stashed our lunch. Peanut butter and jelly always tasted better in the woods, and as we ate, a soft breeze dried our hot, sweaty bodies.

"Now, what do you want to do, Jean?" Gayle asked.

"You know, we've never gone to the other side of the prairie," I said. "Let's walk over there. I'm still too hot and tired to do anything else." When we reached the tall grass in the distance, we saw a small, oval-shaped pond surrounded by cattails, which sat at the bottom of a three-foot slope. The brown water was not at all good for swimming, but when I pushed aside the grass, I saw a rowboat and oars. What a discovery!

"C'mon, Gayle, let's get in and row around the pond."

"I dunno, Jean. It doesn't look too safe to me."

"You're such a scaredy cat. I'm going even if you don't." I slid down the embankment, covering my oxfords with mud, and gingerly stepped into the middle of the boat. It rocked a bit, but I put the oars in the oarlocks, sat down and rowed around the pond. The day was hot and sunny; I loved hearing the bird songs and the sounds of the oars cutting through the water.

"Hey, whaddya doing in my boat?" yelled a male voice from behind me. At first, all I saw was a dark shadow against the sun. I couldn't tell who it was. Again, he shouted, "Whaddya doin' in my boat?" On instinct, I jumped out of the boat and sank to my waist. It took every ounce of energy I had to make it the ten feet back to shore. With each step, I sank a little deeper into the muddy bottom. I crawled up on the bank just in time to see John Bimber, standing with his hands on his hips, scowling down at me. John was several years older than me, a big, burly guy, deep into sports, hunting and cars, someone the kids at school didn't mess with.

I started up the bank and tried to run, but John stood in my way. Spot barked and snarled at him, and I knew she'd attack him if he put one hand on me. "Where do you think you're going?" he said. "You get back in that water and get my goddamn boat you left in the middle of the pond."

"No, I won't," I answered. "It's icky in there." I could not imagine going back into that slimy pit. It had to be full of water moccasins. The bottom might even be quicksand, and I'd end up like the father in *A Girl of Limberlost* who got sucked down and was never seen again. I yelled to Gayle for help. She didn't know what to do; she looked at me wide-eyed and scared. I realized I didn't have a choice but to do as John said. I could not scale the slippery embankment fast enough to get away, so I had to go get his boat.

My first steps back into the mire almost sucked my shoes right off my feet. Slowly, I made it the ten feet or so to the boat, dragged it back to shore and tied it to the stake where I found it. John just stared at me the entire time.

Gayle and I scrambled up the ridge and ran back toward the prairie. I looked back at John as he yelled, "Don't ever come back here again!"

"I hate you John Bimber," I shouted back and ran even faster.

Gayle and I went back to the little stream where I cleaned the mud off my clothes and shoes as much as possible. It was time to head home, and I hoped I could sneak in the side door and get up to my room to change clothes before anyone saw me. *Damn you, John Bimber. I hate it when someone gets the best of me, especially a dumb, old boy like you!*

Conewango Creek

AWARM BREEZE BLEW through my opened bedroom window early one summer morning. I stared out at the swaying leaves of the red maple tree in our yard as the new day's sun peeked through its branches. The only sounds I heard were those of the true early birds, the robins, *cheerily* calling back and forth to one another. That was how their song sounded, *cheerily, cheer up, cheer up, cheerily, cheer up.* This was the best time of the day.

I loved waking up before anyone else in the house, taking out Spot and sitting on the front porch steps in my pajamas, listening to the stillness of the morning and knowing Spot and I were the only ones enjoying the show. Soon the silence would give way to the milkman clanking bottles of fresh milk as he placed them on his customers' front porches, all the dads rushing off to work in their cars, moms banging pots in the kitchen while cooking breakfast, babies crying, and dogs barking. In this time of stillness, I thought about what to do with my day.

"I know. Spot, let's go fishing at the *crick.*" Spot barked and wagged her tail in agreement.

FISHING WAS ONE OF MY favorite things to do. This love began when I was six years old on a trip to Chautauqua Lake in New York near Jamestown. My grandparents on my father's side took me with them to visit relatives, staying on a houseboat for the summer. Grandpa drove the half hour or so to the lake with me asking every few minutes, "Are we there yet?"

After repeating the question a hundred more times, Grandma looked back at me over the tops of her glasses and finally gave me the answer I'd been waiting to hear, "Oh yes, only a few minutes more, Jean." Then I smelled the motorboat fuel and heard the water lapping against the sides of the boats tied to the dock. Grandpa pulled his big, comfy car into a small parking space, and we walked down the dock to our relatives' houseboat.

It was love at first sight. I had never seen a houseboat before, and it was beautiful. It had a small kitchen with a miniature stove, sink and refrigerator, a bathroom they called a head and one big living room and bedroom combined. The idea of sleeping and eating on a boat fascinated me.

Sitting out on the deck, I gazed down at the clear, green water of Chautauqua Lake and breathed in the fishy-kerosene-like smells all around me. I had never seen a lake before, and I thought it was magnificent. Marsh grass and lily pads hugged the shore, the perfect place for fish to hang out on a hot day. I dangled my feet in the water, watching minnows as they nibbled at my toes to see if there was anything good to eat. I saw shadows of larger fish swimming below the minnows, but they were too far down for me to figure out what kind they were.

Heaven had to be just like this place. The blue, summer sky touched the green lake in the distance, and little waves lapped against the side of the boat. The stillness was broken every so often when a speed boat went by, leaving its wake gently rocking the houseboat, but other than that, the only sound was that of the adults quietly talking inside.

Just then, Grandpa's cousin asked me if I wanted to fish. "Oh yes," I exclaimed, so excited I could hardly breathe. The man left for a few minutes and came back with a fishing pole and some worms.

After baiting the hook with a worm, he slowly lowered the line through an eight-inch-hole in the deck. "Now, just sit there and wait for a nibble on your line. If you feel a tug and see the bobber go under, jerk the line, and you just may catch yourself a fish." I felt so grown up, knowing that he trusted me enough to let me use his pole. I held onto that pole like my life depended on it. I sat there fishing for more than an hour with no luck. The fish just kept taking my bait, but I didn't care. I had found a thing I could do forever.

Then...a nibble and another one and another one. I jerked the line like the nice man told me to do and brought in a shining, black and gold pumpkinseed sunfish. It was the most beautiful fish I ever saw, too beautiful to keep, so I let it go to live another day, hoping I could come back some other time and fish again.

I remained quiet on the drive back home, reliving a most wonderful day that my grandparents made possible.

THE WOODS AND THE CRICK

"c'mon, spot. Let's go fishing. We're wasting daylight." I went back inside the house, and everyone was finishing up breakfast and running out the door. Donnie took off to his friend Jack Timmis' house. Daddy left for work. Kaye was helping Mom in the kitchen. After a quick bite, I ran upstairs to put on jeans; I needed the pockets for my fishing stuff.

This was the mid-forties, and girls just didn't wear jeans back then, but my mom was practical, so she bought all us kids jeans. We got so dirty all the time; she figured jeans were the easiest clothes to clean. Maybe we were the ones who got the jean fad started.

After I got my jeans on, I looked around for shoes to wear. I went into Donnie's room to see if he had worn his cowboy boots that day. He hadn't, so I decided I'd borrow them. Cowboy boots were perfect for fishing. Because they were three sizes too big for me, I just stepped into them and shuffled off down the stairs. I didn't care if they were too big; I was in love with those boots.

Almost ready. I packed a couple of sandwiches and then went out to the garage for a shovel. In our yard, we had a pile of old leaves that just disintegrated into dirt. There were plenty of worms for the taking. I filled my can with dirt and worms, got my fishing pole, a couple of extra hooks, sinkers, a bobber and a line to string the fish I caught. Today was a good day; I had everything I needed. Sometimes when I was really desperate, I used bent straight pins for hooks and tied small, flat stones on my line for sinkers. My substitutions didn't work too well, but it was better than not going fishing at all. With all my gear packed up and ready to go, I said goodbye to Mom and headed out the door with Spot.

I looked funny walking in Donnie's boots. Really I could only shuffle along, passing behind the Campbells' house. The path was still wet with the early morning dew and dotted with thorny blackberry bushes. As I got closer to Conewango Creek, the scents of muddy water, fish, and the aptly named skunk cabbage permeated my nostrils. I heard the rushing rapids as I neared the creek and felt the air, laden with moisture. Spot took off on her own, checking the surrounding area for anything to chase, but she never strayed far from me. She was my protector and always let me know if anyone came around us.

When we got to the creek, I took off Donnie's boots, rolled up my jeans as far as they would go, stuffed some worms in my jeans' pocket—I couldn't carry the can and the fish too—and waded off into the rapids. The rapids were only knee high at the deepest, but I still managed to get my jeans soaked. I never figured out how that happened. The fishing here was excellent. I always caught a lot of fish—golden shiners, horned ace, chubs and occasionally at the bottom of the rapids, a sucker or bass, but I enjoyed catching shiners most of all. They swam in large groups and came and went quickly, so when they started hitting my line, it was a lot of fun. When I hooked a shiner, they leaped out of the water, trying to break free, and the sun reflected on their sides, making them look silvery, like a shiny, new coin.

I WAS A TRUE FISHERMAN; I fished rain or shine, as long as there was no thunder and lightning. Once I caught a fish big enough to eat, I waded back to shore and put it on a stringer. I made my stringer by tying some fishing line to a short stick, and then I put the stick through the fish's mouth and out one of its gills. I tied the fishing line to a tree branch, so my catch could swim in the water and not die, but they couldn't get away. Sometimes I stopped fishing long enough to wade around in the shallows, turning over rocks, looking for crawfish, what we called *crabs*. I used crawfish for bait as well as the worms. They really knew how to hide. I had to turn over quite a few rocks to find them. When I did, I shelled them and used only the tails; the fish liked them better that way. I got lucky once in a while and found one shedding his old shell and growing a new one that was still soft all over. Then I used the whole crawfish.

Around noon, I stopped fishing for a bit, sat under a large tree and ate my peanut butter sandwiches. Spot watched every bite I took and waited patiently for her fair share. I always split my lunch with Spot. Sometimes I left a baited line in the water while I ate under a tree not far away, even though I typically didn't catch much in the afternoon. I tried to pull my line up after I finished eating,

MY FAVORITE SPOT

and I thought I had a snag or was caught on an underwater branch. I soon realized I had something on the line. I pulled it up slowly and saw an ugly, brown creature about eighteen inches long with a flat head, teeth like a person, four legs and a tail. I had never seen anything so grotesque in all my life.

A fisherman walking up the path stopped to see what I had as I tried to figure out what to do with it. He looked at the beast on the end of my line and said, "Well, darlin', you got yourself one ugly mudpuppy. Cut the line and let it go. They bite." I gladly did as he said. Later I found out that this creature wasn't a fish at all; it was a salamander that lived in rivers and streams and ate crawfish, worms and snails. Thankfully I never ran into another one of those guys.

Afterwards, I fished for a while longer and decided I had enough for a meal, so I waded back to shore. I checked my legs and feet for bloodsuckers or what some people called leeches. I hated those things. I could never figure out how they crawled up my legs and gorged on my blood without me knowing it. Before I put my boots—well really, Donnie's boots—and socks back on, I took my knife and scraped off a few of them. Disgusting.

Before I left for the day, I took a minute to enjoy one of my favorite places in the whole wide world. I liked to sit in the quiet and listen to the moving water and the wind blowing through the trees. I loved the smell of fish mixed in with fresh dirt and leaves, and the special scent that creeks, rivers, and ponds have. I liked people all right, but sometimes I just wanted to not talk. On those days, Spot was plenty enough company for me.

I gathered up my fishing gear and decided to walk along the shore a bit before going home. When I wasn't fishing, I liked to wade around in the shallows, catching minnows and crawfish, skip flat stones across the water's surface—my record was ten hops—and pick flowers for my mom. That day I headed home with a handful of yellow buttercups and Queen Anne's lace.

The flowers reminded me of one spring when Donnie and I went down to the creek and came across a damp, flat piece of ground, at least a quarter-acre or more, covered in wild violets; it was a sea of purples and lavenders and whites. We spent a couple of hours picking the very best violets for Mom, and we were especially excited when we found her favorites—yellow flowers with purple eyes. Her eyes lit up when we gave them to her, and she couldn't quit *oohing* and *aahing* over them as she hunted up a couple of small vases and put the flowers on the gate-legged table for everyone to see.

WHEN I TOLD SPOT, "C'mon, let's go," she stopped her investigative work and fell in close behind me. We hadn't walked far when Spot suddenly started barking and looking at a boat with three teenaged boys in it fifty feet away from us. I recognized two of them as the Gebhart boys; they lived on the Conewango Avenue Extension. I stopped walking and looked at them warily. I didn't know them, but I had heard about them. They had bad reputations as rough, country boys. Today they all had little grins on their faces; I immediately felt suspicious.

"Good fishin' today? You catch much?" one of the Gebharts asked. I stopped walking and stared at them. I didn't respond.

"Hey, uh," the other brother said, "you want a piece of ass?"

What do they mean? I haven't heard that before. Coming from these guys, it can't be good. "What do you mean?" I asked.

"What I mean is..." the same brother said, "do you want to fuck?'"

I knew what that word meant. I turned around to run, but Donnie's boots, three sizes too big weren't taking me anywhere too fast. C'mon boots, get me outta here! It was like one of those nightmares I had sometimes where everything was in slow motion. I couldn't get any momentum going, and I was sure they were coming after me to do who knows what. The only part of me left would be these damn cowboy boots stuck in the mud!

Spot barked and barked at them while I shuffled up the path as fast as the boots allowed and prayed, *Please God, get me home, and I promise to never wear Donnie's boots again as long as I live.* I'm sure I was a sight—clomping up the path, wearing boots three sizes too big and totally wet jeans, hanging onto my fishing pole and my catch, with Spot, barking and trailing right behind me. I never looked back; I just ran. I probably provided them with a good laugh that day.

Taking flight

HI, JEAN. WHAT YOU DOING?" asked Gayle from the other end of the phone line. My mind raced through all the possibilities. It was Saturday, and the summer sun was bright and warm even at this early hour; it was a day too good to stay around the house.

Even though I had to chores to do each Saturday—clean my bedroom and dust the dreaded table in the dining room—I figured it was worth a try. "Hang on, Gayle," I said into the receiver and put it down on the table. Maybe Mom forgot that today was chore day. "Mom, can I go out with Gayle today?"

"Certainly, Jean" Mom said.

All right, I thought to myself as I bolted toward the phone.

Mom stopped me dead in my tracks when she finished her sentence, "As soon as you get your cleaning done."

"Aw Mom, can't I do it later?" I pleaded.

"Jean, you know the rules. Cleaning comes first, and then you can go play."

I went back to the phone and gave Gayle both the bad news and the good news. "Okay, Gayle. I can go but not until I get my bedroom cleaned and do my chores. It will take about an hour, so pack a lunch and come meet me. I have a great idea where we can go for the day."

"What is it?" Gayle asked.

"Tell you later. I got to go," I said as I hung up the phone and raced off to do my chores.

First off, I had to tackle the gate-leg table in the dining room. I hated that thing. It was old and rickety, and it had way more legs than a normal table,

MY DREAM HORSE

just that much more to dust. When we weren't using it, the eight legs and parts of the table top folded in on itself, so it didn't take up a lot of room. And that was the way it stayed. We never used it for dinner or anything; it just sat in the living room looking pretty with a scarf on top of it. We didn't even use it for Christmas dinner, though Mom did put decorations on it. For some reason, Mom loved that thing, so I had to dust it every week and do a good job, or she'd make me do it again. To me, it was just a pain, too many places for dust to collect. I used oil to clean all the knobs on the legs and tried to make them squeak in different tones just to entertain myself. This table was a waste of good daylight.

I finally finished with the table and ran upstairs to deal with my bedroom. I hung my clothes, picked up the latest Nancy Drew mystery I had been reading, and put away the tablets of my latest horse drawings. I had been sketching some new ones all morning when I was *supposed* to be cleaning up my room. Just in case Mom came in to check, I swept all the other stuff on the floor under the bed, made my bed and swished the dust cloth over everything. I took one final look, turned off the light and ran downstairs to make a couple of peanut butter sandwiches to take with me. I was finally *free!* I ran out the kitchen door, slamming it behind me, and raced down the street to meet Gayle halfway up the block, ready for the day's adventure.

As soon as I saw Gayle, I said, "I have a great idea of what we can do today."

"Tell me, tell me," Gayle asked, clapping her hands. We had been friends since we were in the first grade, and she liked to have fun just like me.

"Well, I thought we could go to Evelyn Lindsey's house."

"Evelyn Lindsey? Who's that?" Gayle asked, pulling her reddish-brown hair back in a ponytail.

"Silly, we're not going to see Evelyn. We're going see Cotton." Cotton was the white, part-Arabian pony my uncle had rented for me once. Cotton had a long mane and tail, and I wished I could have seen him in his prime when he reared up and walked around the circus ring on his hind legs. He was retired now and too old to do that anymore. I rode him sometimes when I had enough money to rent him for an hour or so. He was a wonderful horse, easy to handle, and he still reared up on command. I loved him dearly.

"Ooooh, that sounds like fun," Gayle said. "Let's get going."

I HOPED THIS VISIT to Lindsey's farm would be better than the last. On my previous trip, I had seen a bunch of teenaged girls washing or brushing the horses, bridling them and mucking out the stalls. I walked over and started talking, trying to convince them to let me ride.

Repeatedly they asked, "Are you sure you know how to ride?"

I acted insulted and said, "Of course, I know how." In truth, I had only been on a horse a couple of times in my whole life.

"Well okay," the girl with the long blond hair flowing out from under her cowboy hat answered. "I'll put a bridle on Steel and let you take him around the field."

I couldn't believe my good luck. Steel was a *huge*, dapple-gray gelding. He stood sixteen hands high, and I could tell he was full of spunk as he pranced around, side-stepping and pawing the ground. The girl leaned against the horse and cupped her hands for my foot to give me a step up onto Steel's back. When this girl slapped Steel on the rear, I was off and galloping around the field.

For a few seconds, it was the ride of a lifetime. Suddenly, Steel stepped into a groundhog hole, and I went flying over his head and hit my head hard on the ground. Steel fell, too, and rolled over.

The girls ran over to see if I was okay, and luckily, neither of us was seriously hurt. "Hey, you know if you don't get right back on that horse after you fall, you're going to be afraid and never ride again."

That certainly wasn't going to happen to me; no horse was going to get the best of me. So I got up and brushed the dirt off my clothes and gingerly crawled back onto Steel's back with the girls' help. I walked him around the field with no more mishaps, but because of the pounding headache I had, it was a short ride.

THIS TIME WILL BE BETTER, I told myself.. Our destination, the Southside, was about two miles away. To get there, we had to go through downtown Warren, across the Alleghany River Bridge, past the cemetery and up the dirt road to Evelyn's house, but we didn't take a direct route. We made a few detours and had things to do along the way. In the front window of Brown's Shoe Store, I made sure the loafers I had been looking at for weeks were still there. They were dark brown with white and brown horsehair on the top, and I had almost saved enough money to buy them. Then we went by the Bette Dixon Candy Store to see if she was giving out free samples. She wasn't. I didn't have enough money today, but whenever I did, I always bought a dark chocolate, butter cream candy. Yummy!

We then checked out the fish in the river under the Southside Bridge. Some days the water was too muddy to see anything, but this morning we spied carp, suckers, bass and catfish with their long whiskers. We picked up a couple of rocks and tried to hit a fish, but they were too fast for us. *One day, we'll get them.*

Then we had to look at the old tombstones on the way past the Southside Cemetery. "I wonder who's buried there, Gayle," I said. "There isn't any writing on it anymore. It's all worn away."

"They must have been dead for a long time," Gayle added. "Jean, I'm hungry."

"Okay, let's go over there to eat," I said. We settled down in the grass under a big oak tree and began devouring our peanut butter sandwiches. The peanut butter stuck to the roofs of our mouths, and to make things worse, we were in such a hurry to get out of our houses, we both forgot to bring along something to drink.

ONCE WE RESUMED OUR TREK, Gayle asked, "Are we almost there, Jean? I'm really hot and sweaty."

"Just a little bit farther," I answered. "It will be worth it when you see Cotton." Finally we went around a bend in the road, and there was the Lindsey's farm. A white, clapboard farmhouse sat on the left of the road, and the huge, grey barn was across the street. It had a white-board fence corralling the horses and cattle. Gayle and I ran and climbed up on the fence, straining our eyes to catch a glimpse of Cotton. He was nowhere to be found. "Let's check the barn," I said.

We didn't see anyone around to ask, so we walked cautiously through the big, open doors. I smelled it before I saw it—the sweet, grassy scent of newly mowed hay. I loved that smell. All around the area, farmers harvested hay for the last time of the summer. The barn was filled with hay—huge piles, some as big as houses, some in bales and some loose hay scattered around on the floor. We looked around to see what else was in there besides the hay. No Cotton.

"Jeez, Jean," Gayle said, pointing up to the rafters, "look at the rope swing. I have to swing from that." She hustled up the mounds of hay and straddled the big knot tied at the end of the rope. With a big push, she swung out over the barn floor. "Wheeee, this is fun!" she yelled down to me as I watched her fly back and forth, straining her body to go higher and higher.

I kept looking back over my shoulder to see if anyone was coming. At one point, I saw an old farmer dressed in dirty blue overalls and a gray work shirt coming toward the barn. He was stooped over and walked real slow and stiff-like. As he got closer and closer, Gayle kept swinging up into the rafters.

"Gayle, get off the swing. Somebody's coming, and I don't know who he is." I said. "Maybe we shouldn't be in here." Gayle scampered down the hay bales, and we stood side-by-side, awaiting our fate.

"Well, hello there," the man said in a gruff voice as he approached us. "I'm Mr. Lindsey, Evelyn's grandfather. What are you little girls doing here?

The words tumbled out of my mouth, "We came to see Cotton, and we couldn't find him anywhere. We thought he might be in the barn. Once we got inside, we saw the rope swing and just had to try it out."

Mr. Lindsey chuckled. "Evelyn's not here right now, and Cotton is rented out for the day, but you can certainly swing." Gayle and I squealed in delight. He continued, "Look, I'll sit right here on this bale of hay and keep an eye on you, so you don't get hurt, okay?"

What a nice man, I thought to myself. *He didn't get mad at us for being in here without permission, and now he's letting us swing and making sure we don't hurt ourselves.*

"Now you, little girl," he said, pointing to me, "you come sit on my lap and watch your friend swing. Then it will be your turn." Gayle jumped on the swing and slowly began to gain altitude. I walked over and climbed up on his lap, looking up at Gayle on the swing. I felt strange sitting on the lap of a man I didn't know, but he seemed nice, and I really wanted to try out that swing.

I hadn't been sitting on Mr. Lindsey's lap for very long when I felt his hands on my eleven-year-old chest. Even though there wasn't much there, I knew he shouldn't be doing that. I shifted my weight over a little, and he pulled away his hand. I relaxed somewhat, but then his hands slowly went down to my crotch. I jumped off his lap and yelled to Gayle, "Hey, it's my turn to swing."

Gayle slid off the swing and went over to sit in Mr. Lindsey's lap. I wrapped my legs around the rope and began to swing, but I didn't enjoy it. I kept looking over at Gayle. I swung back and forth for a couple of minutes, but I felt uncomfortable with the situation and decided we should leave. "Okay, Gayle, time to go home now," I said. I knew she didn't want to leave, but she followed me as I walked out of the barn.

"Goodbye girls. I'm going home, too," the old man said, as we scurried out of the barn. "Come back anytime you want to swing."

Walking down the dirt road toward home, I asked Gayle, "Did that old man do anything to you, like touch you where he shouldn't?"

"No, he didn't do anything," she replied. Her mind drifted back to the barn, "Golly that was fun swinging on that rope swing."

We looked behind us and saw Mr. Lindsey walking across the road to the farmhouse. "I know. That was really fun. Let's go back for a couple more swings." We ran to the barn, making sure he wasn't coming back.

Gayle climbed onto the rope and sailed back and forth, back and forth through the air, higher and higher each time. All of a sudden, I heard the crunching of gravel and got scared that Mr. Lindsey was coming back to the barn. "Gayle, quick, jump off and run up into the haymow, now!" I screamed. Running as fast as the hay on the barn floor would allow and looking back to see if he was coming, I turned around and smacked my forehead on one of the huge rafters. I flipped over backwards, somersaulted and landed on my stomach with a mouthful of hay. I felt stunned and dizzy, so I lay there for a moment to get my bearings.

"Jean, are you all right?" Gayle asked.

"Yeah, yeah...I think I'm okay." I felt the beginnings of a big bump already. *Oh boy, this is going to be a good one. Thankfully, there's no blood.* "It's time to go home now. I've had my fill of swinging. That old man hasn't come back yet, so let's get out of here before he does," I said. "I didn't like him at all. We'll see Cotton another day." But I never went back to that farm.

Conewango Dam Adventure

HEY, JANET. Want to go fishing at the dam this morning?" I asked my friend on the other end of the phone. It was a beautiful, summer morning—the perfect day to catch a big fish. Usually I didn't mind fishing alone, but I had never been fishing at the Conewango Dam on the Conewango Avenue extension, so I didn't want to go by myself. I figured two people were better than one just in case anything happened.

"Uh, let me ask," Janet said. I listened to the muffled sounds as she talked with her mom while holding her hand over the receiver. I first thought of asking Norma to go fishing, but she always had chores to do, which took up most of the morning. I didn't want to wait until the afternoon because everybody knows the biggest fish bite in the morning. Janet spoke into the receiver, "Okay, Jeannie, I can go."

"Pack some sandwiches and a drink. We'll be gone most of the day," I said. "Come over in a half hour. I have to go out back and dig up some worms."

JANET SHOWED UP with her fishing gear, but when I went to the garage to get a bike, both were already gone. Kaye and Donnie must have used the two bikes we shared to go visit friends. *Oh well, I'll have to ride with Janet. When she gets tired, I'll walk.*

We headed up Conewango Avenue, stopped at Churchill's Grocery for sodas and continued north for about a mile to the dam. When we arrived, there were no other fishermen in sight. *Great! More fish for us.* We took a dirt road down a slight incline of two hundred feet or so to get to the dam.

The low head, concrete dam stretched across Conewango Creek and had a spillway with a good flow of water moving through it, so we stood on the dam and fished near the chute. Each end of the dam had a concrete wall and a flat area where we kept our lunches and drinks out of the sun.

Once we got settled, we baited our hooks, walked out onto the dam and threw our fishing lines down river into the current. The water level was low, so we sat on the dam and waited for a bite, enjoying the warm, summer morning and the slight breeze blowing through our hair.

The fish kept taking our bait, so the hours passed slowly. We ate our lunch and drank our sodas and still had not caught a fish worth keeping. "Jeez, Janet, where are all the fish? Maybe we should use a whole worm next time," I said. The night crawlers we had were twelve inches long, so we usually cut them in half before baiting our hooks.

We had the dam to ourselves all morning, but that afternoon we heard a vehicle coming down the dirt road and saw a black pickup truck pull into the parking lot. A short man with a bald head and a big belly got out of the truck and walked down to the dam. Janet and I didn't pay much attention to him; our focus was on catching a fish we could keep. The next time we looked up, the man had disappeared from sight, but his truck remained in the parking lot.

"Jeannie, I'm going get another soda. Be back in a minute," Janet said. I finally had a nibble and was watching my line closely when Janet came right back, leaned over and whispered in my ear, "Jeannie, that man in the black truck is sitting by our stuff with his *dink* hanging out of his bathing suit!"

"Yeah, sure, Janet. Tell me another one," I said, figuring she was up to her old tricks of making me believe things that weren't true.

"No, really, Jeannie, honest to God. Go see for yourself if you don't believe me."

I pulled myself up and slowly walked over to the side. I looked over at the man while I reached for a drink. Janet was right. That man was just sitting there with his own big worm hanging out like it was no big deal. The sight of his privates disgusted me; I had never seen one before and didn't want to now. He didn't look at me or make any attempt to cover himself up. I slowly walked back to where Janet was.

"We have to get out of here, *now*," I said to Janet, "but he can't see us leaving." Being as quiet as possible, we scooped up our fishing poles and stayed as far away from him as we could. Janet jumped on her bike, and I took off running up the dirt road to Conewango Avenue.

The man looked around, saw us running away, raced to his truck and came after us. Having only one bike created a big problem. With me on foot, he could easily get to me. There weren't many houses on that part of Cone-wango, so as Janet headed down the road on her bike, I ran to the first house on the right and pounded on the door. Unfortunately no one was home, so I started running again, looking back over my shoulder to see where the man was. Janet then turned her bike around and came back to get me, so I hopped on the back, and we took off. Just a little ways down the road, we saw him coming towards us. I stared at him as he went by, memorizing every detail of his determined face.

By the time he found a place to turn around, we had made it into town. Janet and I breathed a sigh of relief as we ran to our houses. I threw open the side door of my house, calling for my mom. I told her the whole story in between gasping for breath, and she immediately called my dad at his job. Then she called the police. "Now, Jean, don't be afraid," my mom said after she hung up the phone. "The police want to catch the bad man, and you need to answer all of their questions." She knew how difficult it was going to be for me to tell a complete stranger such embarrassing things. I paced around the house and tried to think of anything else until I heard the knock on our front door. He didn't look like a policeman to me. He had on regular clothes and was real friendly. I sat down in one chair, and he pulled up another one and began asking questions.

I told him everything. He was particularly interested in the part about the man sitting on the shelf with his bathing suit pulled aside. I think he wanted to make sure it was deliberate, not just an embarrassing mistake. Once I finished my story, he was convinced. I didn't catch the man's license plate number, so there wasn't a whole lot he could do. He went over to the Carlson's house to talk with Janet next, but her parents refused to allow him to talk with her. I figured they just wanted the whole thing to go away.

TWO WEEKS LATER, my friend Norma and I rode our bikes up the Conewango Avenue extension. When we passed the dam, I saw that same black truck drive past us going south. "Norma," I yelled, "that's the man I told you about, the one who showed himself to Janet and me. We need to get to a phone and call my mom, quick." We pedaled as fast as we could to the first house we came to, turned into the driveway and threw down our bikes. When I pounded on the front door, a lady named Mrs. Gebhart let us in. I got my mom on the phone and told her where I was and what was going on.

"Jean, stay where you are, and your Uncle Glenn and I will walk up Cone-wango to you. Don't go anywhere," she said.

We waited and waited, at least fifteen minutes. No Mom and Uncle Glenn. I just had to get home where I felt safe. Finally, Norma and I decided to make a run for it on our bikes. We pulled out of Mrs. Gebhart's driveway and raced down the road. The man in the black truck passed us again, going the other way. Norma and I took our bikes and hid behind a huge boulder five feet off the road on the left-hand side of the Fishers' house.

"Jeannie, I'm scared," Norma whispered, as she tried to catch her breath.

"Yeah," I nodded, but I really didn't have time to think about that right now. I knew the only way for police to catch this guy was to get his license plate number, so I picked up a flat piece of shale and a rock and waited. At just the right time, I jumped out from behind the boulder, ran to the side of the road and wrote down the number as he went by again. I stuck the shale in my pocket, and Norma and I raced down the road. We ran into Mom, my sister Linda and Uncle Glenn coming up the road to get us. They had been walking toward the house of another Gebhart family on Quaker Hill Road. With the license number, I got the man.

I NEVER KNEW what came of him after he was arrested, but years later when my dad and I attended a Drum and Bugle Corps competition on the Fourth of July in Warren, I saw the man who chased me. I pointed him out to my dad. Dad just looked at me for a few moments and said, "You know, Jean, I worried for years that maybe you accused the wrong man, but when you pointed that guy out to me, it was such a relief. You really did get your man." Then he wrapped his arms around me and gave me a big hug.

Sly Like a Fox

ONE SATURDAY MORNING in October 1945, I looked out my bedroom window to see nothing but gray—gray skies, bare gray trees, dead gray grass. *What will I do to liven up this dreary day?* My four-legged best friend Spot sat and looked up at me with her head cocked to one side, waiting patiently for the plan. She knew my adventures always included her.

I got wind of horses being kept in a field at the fox farm, and I wanted to see them. I had never been to the fox farm before, so I had no idea of what was there. I always looked for new adventures. My brother Donnie was off somewhere with his friends, so Spot and I decided to go alone.

I stuck my nose out the front door to check the temperature and was met with a blast of cold air that made me jump back into the living room and slam the door shut. *Brrrrrrr, Spot. It's cold out there. We better bundle up.* I put on a thick shirt, sweater, winter jacket, kerchief on my head and galoshes for our trek through the woods along Quaker Hill Road to the fox farm. Spot already had on her thick, winter coat.

I told Mom and Dad goodbye, saying I was going out for a walk with Spot. Opening the kitchen door just a crack, the raw, cutting wind was even stronger than I expected, and the gray skies made the day seem gloomy. But Spot and I were starting out on an adventure, and any old kind of day was a good one for exploring.

The trip to the fox farm was about a mile long and mostly uphill. We traveled from Kenmore Street, took a short left then a right on Connecticut Avenue to the top of the hill and made a left on Edgewood Place, a right on Quaker Hill Road and climbed up the bank into the forest of oak, pine, and red maple trees draped in wild grapevines. A path ran along the edge of the dense woods where deer, bear, wild turkey, and a host of other small animals roamed. In season, hunters traveled the same road. By this time in October, the leaves had all fallen and lay on the ground like a gray-brown carpet. They crunched beneath my feet as I slowly walked uphill, intently listening for the sounds of wild animals or other people, but all I heard were bird calls and the barks of squirrels.

Spot scouted the hillside, looking for rabbits and squirrels to chase. She perked up her ears, so she wouldn't miss a sound. *What do you hear, girl? Go get 'em!* And off she'd go, tearing through the woods in hot pursuit of some unsuspecting creature. Spot was my lookout and kept me aware of any danger. She let me know if people were around way before they actually saw us. I felt safe with her by my side.

Even with Spot's protection, I was a little unnerved on this day. The lack of color and the strong, cold wind made me uneasy. I jumped when the wind sent a limb crashing to the ground or rustled the dead leaves around me. Still, Spot and I pressed on. At one point, I sat on a fallen log to rest and saw how the trees and animals prepared for the cold, drab winter months ahead. The squirrels scurried about, looking for any leftover acorns they could stash in holes for later. In the distance, a doe stood quietly and looked in my direction. Her coat was thick; it was going to be a long winter. I wondered if they also looked forward to a bright, spring day as I did.

Ten minutes farther up the trail, we came to the end of the path and found a house and barn. Many cages were stacked up inside a fenced-in area down the road on the left. On the other side of the road was a large pasture. *That is probably where they keep the horses.* Spot and I walked to the edge of the field, and I strained my eyes to find them. Finally I saw some at the far side of the field, and I started whinnying until one began walking in my direction. Before long, all three of the horses stood at the fence, looking for a handout. I hadn't brought anything with me, so I grabbed the few blades of green grass I could find and gave them that. These horses were so skinny that I could see ribs poking out of their sides. Their manes and tails were all matted, and their coats had big, bare spots. Their lower lips hung down, and even their eyes looked dull.

After eating the few blades of grass I managed to find, they bored of my paltry attempts and walked back into the field. I felt sad seeing them in such bad shape and looking so old. *If they were my horses, I'd certainly take better care of them than this.*

Curiosity got the best of me, and I decided to investigate the other side of the road where all the cages were. I walked down to the entrance of the fenced-in area where two men leaned against the railing, deep in conversation. I smelled the foxes as I neared the cages. It was a strong, musky odor, just shy of stinking like a skunk. It kind of burned my nose. Peering into the cages, I saw red foxes and some gray ones, but they all had beady, black eyes and sharp, pointy black noses. They were all curled up at the back of the wire cages, trying to hide. When anyone approached, they hissed and pressed themselves against the wire. I felt sorry for them. Keeping them penned up like this was cruel.

"Hey, little girl. What can we do for ya?" the taller of the two men said. He looked like a big dog with the cap he wore. It had ear flaps that were blowing around in the wind.

"I came to see the horses," I said as I looked them over. They both wore overalls, plaid, wool shirts and rubber boots.

The man with the cap was real friendly. "Come over here, little girl, and let me see ya." I slowly walked over to him, and he picked me up in his arms, which was easy to do. I was thin and wiry and probably weighed all of sixty pounds. "How 'bout a little kiss, right here on the cheek?" I gave him a little peck, but then he asked me to do it again.

"I think I want down," I said.

He put me back on the ground and said, "Listen, little girl, we have some really nice horses in the barn. Would you like to see them?" I tried to not look at him. "They are right there, down the road on the right." The barn looked harmless enough; it had a big open door, was close to the main road and next to the farmhouse. I looked at Spot, and she didn't seem too worried. She was busy sniffing around, looking for some animal to chase. I really wanted to see some nice horses, so I nodded my head and said okay.

I followed him to the barn. He went in first. I stood at the door, looking into the yawning blackness. It was so dark, I couldn't even see him. Something told me this was a dangerous place, so I held back for just a moment or two.

All of a sudden, a loud voice from the house next to the barn shouted, "Frank...Frank, I need you back at the fox cages. Now!"

The man with the floppy-eared cap called back, "Okay, boss, be right there," and started walking back to the cages. "Listen, little girl, you have to leave now. Come back another time, okay?"

I took off like a shot, running down that cold, windy hill with Spot right beside me, feeling like I had been rescued by someone I never saw. I ran all the way home. Once I made it back to my nice, warm house, I tore off my coat and galoshes and took a big breath. I never felt so glad to be in our kitchen.

A few days later, I learned a lot more about the fox farm. I found out that the horses were killed to feed the foxes, and the foxes were killed for their fur, which was used for coats, stoles, hats, collars, and cuffs. Even more chilling for me, a girlfriend's fourteen-year-old sister had been chased by someone a block from my house only a few nights before. She ran to a neighbor's house and pounded on the front door until someone let her in and called the police. When officers caught her attacker, it was the same man I nearly went into the barn with that day at the fox farm. Someone— I'll never know how or who—saved me that day.

What to Do on a Winter's Day?

FALL TURNED TO WINTER quickly in Warren, and when the temperature dropped our activities moved indoors. My sister, brother and I listened intently to the evening news as the weather man predicted heavy storms—snow three feet deep with five-foot drifts—and informed us that school would be closed the next day. Cheers rang throughout the house.

Happy I didn't have anywhere to go in the morning, I snuggled under the warm covers of my bed to dream. *Tonight my mount is a white stallion, taking me through the snow, kicking up clouds of white behind us as we charge through the drifts and we patrol the streets of Warren, looking for evildoers.*

THE MORNING light crept into the bedroom. I opened my eyes to see snowflakes hitting the windows and covering the roof with a lovely carpet of white. Snow piled high on the limbs of the ma-

KENMORE STREET

SPOT DOING TRICKS IN THE SNOW

ple tree and made everything look like a picture postcard.

I crawled out of bed, wrapped my robe around me, and tip-toed downstairs where I found Spot waiting for me. I opened the door just a crack and let her out to do her business. She didn't go far because she was short and had to leap through the deep snow; she disappeared with every jump. Quickly she found the best spot, which was always in Mrs. Hayes' yard. That was Spot's territory whether the old lady liked it or not. The cold air made me shiver, and after letting Spot back into the house, I sat on the heat register in the dining room to get warm. The house was especially cold in the mornings because Dad turned the thermostat down for the night.

Not long after I heard stirring upstairs, Mom came down to make coffee and breakfast and pack Dad's lunch—usually roast beef, bologna, or cheese sandwiches and fruit. I followed her into the kitchen, waiting to see what tasty thing she might fix us this morning. "What would you like to eat, Jean?" Mom asked. "I'm making eggs for Dad. Do you want one?"

"Sure," I answered, "that would be good." One egg was yummy, but a second egg made me gag. One was my limit. I used my two pieces of toast and dipped into the center of my over-easy, fried egg. I loved to watch Dad eat his eggs. He slipped the fork under the first egg and popped the whole thing into his mouth without breaking the yolk. Then he did the same thing with the second egg. It was really neat.

Spot sat quietly out of the way, waiting for her bite of toast. Mom and Dad had strict rules; Spot was not allowed in the room when we were eating, so she always sat in the doorway on high alert.

Dad went off to work, and after waking my baby sister Linda, Mom busied herself with daily chores. Soon Kaye and Donnie got up, so the whole house was awake. No one slept late in our home, even on weekends. Dad was always up before dawn, and he immediately cranked up the record player downstairs. We always woke up to the smooth sounds of Bing Crosby,

Mario Lanza and Frank Sinatra, unless it was December, then we heard non-stop Christmas music.

After breakfast, I went upstairs, dressed, and brushed my teeth while thinking about how to amuse myself for the day. Donnie was in his room reading, and Kaye was downstairs helping Mom with chores. Just like Kaye; she *never* did anything wrong. Mom always said she should have stopped after Kaye. As a kid, I had no idea what she meant by that.

JEAN'S PAPER DOLL CLOTHES

I grabbed a couple of cardboard boxes from the basement and decided to make a dollhouse. I then gathered up everything I might need—scissors from Mom's sewing kit, glue, spare pieces of fabric to cover the doll bed I planned to build. Moving to the corner of the dining room, I spread out all my stuff and went to work. I finished the house in a couple of hours and sat my paper dolls in the chairs I made. I had store-bought paper dolls, but I hand-made their clothes. I traced the doll's outline on white paper—sometimes construction paper—and then colored their dresses, blouses, and pants with crayons or colored pencils. I had a great imagination with clothing styles. Pleased with my accomplishment, I contemplated what to do next.

On the floor a few feet away, I spotted a small object. *Hmmmmm,* I wondered, *what's that? Looks like a hairpin. Why yes, it is one of Mom's.* I reached over, picked it up and studied it for a while and thought about what I could do with it. I glanced to the left and saw an electric wall socket just sitting there. The hairpin looked like it would fit just fine, so I leaned over and inserted the pin into the socket. *Eeeeeeeeooooooooooow!* The jolt of the electricity shot up my arm and threw me backward on the floor. It took a few minutes for me to recover, and by that time, Mom had walked in to see what was wrong. When I explained what I had done, she didn't know what to do with herself. She was so relieved I was not hurt, but she was also so angry that I did such a stupid thing. She took one of the dining room chairs, placed it in the corner and made me sit there for more than an hour, thinking about the serious thing I had done. I considered just how dangerous my curiosity could be and how I needed to be more careful. I didn't forget the lesson; that shock really, really hurt!

ONE WINTER MORNING, I got up early, way before anyone else, and the bathroom was so cold. I decided to light a fire in the small, gas stove to warm up the room, so I grabbed the box of kitchen matches from the shelf. Our bathroom was about six by nine feet and had a row of four small windows, running across the far wall, which were covered with white gauze curtains. A gap in the lower corner of one window created a draft when the wind blew. I pulled a match out of the box and lit the heater. Then I got bright idea to let the wind from this draft blow out the match. I placed the flame right in front of the little gap at the corner of the window. *Whoosh.* The gauze curtains flamed up in less than a second. *Oh my God, what have I done?* I threw open the bathroom door and bolted into Mom and Dad's bedroom. "The bathroom curtains are on fire! The curtains are on fire!" They flew out of bed and into the bathroom, grabbed towels and beat out the flames.

We had smoke-stained windows and a blackened ceiling but no serious damage thanks to my parents knowing how to put out the fire. Surprisingly, not much was said to me after I explained my lame excuse about how the fire happened. I figured I'd be in the corner for the rest of my life, but I guess they thought, from the look of horror on my face, that the shock was punishment enough. I always seemed to learn my lessons the hard way.

I wasn't a bad kid; I was just curious and wanted to know how things worked. I didn't always think through what I was about to do, and sometimes, that landed me back in the corner. I was no stranger to the corner for making bad decisions, but I was surprised years later when Mom told me about the time she got in trouble when she was a little girl. She was misbehaving in front of company and would not stop. Her mother took her from the room and left her alone, sitting in a dark closet as punishment. After what seemed like ages to her, her mother opened the door and asked what she had been doing, had she learned her lesson. My young mother sneered and said, "I spit in your shoes. I spit in your rubbers. I spit in your boots, and I'm just waiting for more spit!" Her confession convinced me I was more like my mother than I could have imagined.

Winter in Warren

WARREN'S SNOWY WINTERS brought a new set of adventures. Snow blanketed the landscape, and temperatures routinely dipped below thirty-two degrees. When Donnie and I weren't in school, we spent as much time outdoors as our bodies allowed. We went inside only when our feet got so cold it felt as though we were walking on golf balls. At home, when we stripped off our boots and as many as three pairs of socks; we cried out as the prickly needle-like pain shot through our thawing feet. We sat on the heat register in the dining room until we had forgotten all about the cold and our frozen feet. Then we went back outside and did it all over again.

One Christmas, Donnie and I received snow skis and poles. Approximately two feet of fresh snow fell that very day, so we decided to try out our new skis on the hill behind the Old Ladies Home. We trudged up the hill off Quaker Hill Road alongside the woods, not to disturb the pristine, powdery snow covering the slope.

LINDA RIDING A SNOW HORSE

JEAN AT THIRTEEN YEARS OLD — 1948

"Beat you to the bottom," Donnie called out as he raced to put on his skis. We slid our feet into a ribbed piece of rubber and then buckled a leather strap that supposedly kept the skis attached. It didn't work. We made it no farther than five yards before our feet slipped out of the skis, and we fell down. Then the poles got in our way, so we threw them aside. Finally, we made it to the bottom of the hill, exhausted, but we climbed back up and tried again and again. Not only were we covered in snow, but we had cakes of it between our skis and shoes. Our feet slipped off the skis as soon as we started down the hill, and we tumbled head over heels to the bottom. I looked back up the hill, and said to Donnie, "I'm going home. I'm cold and wet, and I have golf balls under my feet." Donnie gave up as well and began walking home. All my thoughts focused on that nice, warm register in the dining room, knowing I was going to be the first to thaw out, no matter what.

MY MOM OWNED a pair of stadium boots, thick leather ankle boots lined with sheep's wool to keep her feet toasty. They had flat leather soles that were slippery on snow and ice, but for sitting in a stadium, watching a football game, they were great. Since my mother didn't go to sporting events, she allowed me to wear her boots once in a while. I didn't go to football games either, but I loved using those stadium boots to slide down Alexander Street when it was really cold, and the road was icy.

Alexander Street was a few blocks from my house and situated on an especially steep hill. When the temperature dropped and the road iced over, few cars even attempted to make it up Alexander Street, so I had it all to myself. I borrowed Mom's stadium boots, and Spot and I made our way over to Alexander Street. Repeatedly, I tried to slide down the hill without falling. It took me six or seven tries, but eventually, I made it all the way to the bottom standing up while Spot ran alongside me and barked encouragement. I never told anyone about that special place; only Spot and I knew the secret of what was possible there. After conquering Alexander Street, I walked home triumphantly, knowing something that no one else did.

ANOTHER CHRISTMAS, we all received ice skates—white figure skates for Kaye and me, black hockey skates for Donnie. Our hometown of Warren did not have many lakes and ponds for us to skate on, so we didn't get a great deal of practice. It took a few times out on the ice to strengthen our ankles and not be so wobbly on the thin blades. Until then, we spent most of our time skating on our inside ankles before we retrained ourselves in the proper way to glide across the ice. Not long after we got the hang of skating, we found Skinner's Pond on the south side of Warren. Gayle or Norma's parents often ran us out there on a weekend night when it was cold enough to skate. The owners charged a small fee to use the one-acre pond and played music by Patsy Cline, Jim Reeves, and Marty Robins for us to skate by. They also had an old shack with a wooden plank floor and a potbellied stove, so when our feet started to freeze, we crowded into the little building to warm up. The scent of damp wool and sweaty bodies filled the hut.

Most of us struggled to skate around the pond, so there were always piles of kids who had fallen on the ice; we either navigated around them or added to the size of the heap. A few good skaters came to Skinner's Pond. One was Patti Larsen. Patti glided onto the ice in her little skating skirt that showed off her perfect legs and wore a short jacket with a hood edged in white rabbit fur. She floated over the ice and effortlessly did spins and figure eights without ever falling. I watched and felt so jealous of her ability to skate. I wanted to be just like her.

After I improved a bit, one of the older guys—he was at least five or six years older—asked me to skate with him. At only 5' 8", he wasn't very tall but was muscular, had movie-star looks and a great smile. Plus, he was a really graceful skater. I felt so flattered that he asked me to go around the pond with him, but my knees were shaking. I felt so clumsy. Everything was fine at first, but then he turned around, so I could skate backwards. Big mistake. I knew how to skate backwards, but I wasn't good at making the switch. My skate caught in his, and we both went down hard, but he got the worst of it. He struggled to his feet and limped off the ice. He must have left because I didn't see him the rest of the night. I felt bad. He was really nice looking, but he was too old for me anyway.

ONE MORNING IN THE MIDDLE of winter, Donnie came into my bedroom and said he had a great idea. "Why don't we skate to school this morning?" I sat up in bed to hear more. "It's been way below freezing the last few days, and the *crick* is frozen," Donnie said. "We could skate all the way to school." It sounded like a super idea to me, but of course, Mom knew nothing about our plan. She always went back to bed after she fixed Dad's breakfast and put our cereal in the double boiler.

Donnie and I got ready for school, bundled up in our warmest clothes, slung our ice skates over our shoulders, grabbed our books and walked down the street to the *crick*. As we thought, the *crick* was frozen solid and had little snow on its surface to interfere with smooth skating. We sat on a log on the bank and laced up our skates.

We skimmed across the ice, the quiet broken only by the swish of our blades as they cut into the frozen surface. Looking like dragons, we breathed in the cold morning air and exhaled plumes of water vapor. Icicles hung from tree limbs lining the bank and sparkled in the bright sunlight. We arrived at the school invigorated by our morning's adventure, stored our skates in our lockers and went off to class.

All day long, I dreamed of skating back home and how much more fun we'd have. When the last bell sounded, I raced to my locker, grabbed my skates and ran down to the *crick* for the skate home. My face fell as soon as I got there. The warm sunlight and rising temperatures had melted the ice along the creek banks, making it unsafe to skate. I turned around and made the slow walk back home to my room, my drawings, and my dreams.

WE HAD BAD RAINSTORMS one winter, and the overflow of the *crick* created small pools of water near its banks that froze hard when the temperature dropped below freezing. Donnie knew of one of these small ponds behind the Samuelsons' house that we could use to ice skate, so we grabbed our skates and a couple of shovels to remove snow from a storm the night before and went to check it out. Of course, Spot came along to see what she could scare out of the bushes.

We followed the path behind Samuelson's garage, and once we arrived at the *crick*, Donnie located the edge of the pond. We began shoveling snow, and our private skating pond grew larger and larger as we cleared the area, revealing a surface like glass. I stopped shoveling for a moment to catch my breath. Donnie did not know I was standing right behind him as he scooped a shovelful of snow and threw it over his shoulder. The corner of the shovel hit me near my eye, and blood spurted out everywhere. I thought sure I was both bleeding to death and going blind. Donnie stood there in shock as I screamed,

"I'm blind! I'm blind! I'm bleeding to death." I stumbled up the hill and rushed home with Spot right beside me. Donnie was so scared, he ran away.

I burst into the house and screamed, "Mom, I can't see out of my eye. I'm blind!"

Mom grabbed a wet cloth, wiped away the blood and found a one-inch cut right below my left eyebrow. "You're all right, Jean. It's not your eye. You do have a pretty good gash. What in the world happened?" I explained what we were doing and told her Donnie got scared and ran away. She examined the cut and concluded, "Well, maybe you should have that cut stitched up."

"No, no, Mom," I yelled, "I don't want to go to the doctor. No, please no."

"I'm going to call your dad and see what he thinks." She went to the phone, and I heard her murmuring. I couldn't make out what she said, but when I saw a slight smile, I figured Dad said I didn't have to go. "It will probably heal all right, but you're going to have a small scar." I hugged her and Spot, too, who had been standing beside me the entire time and seemed to understand what was going on.

Poor Donnie showed up an hour or so later and said he was sorry, that he didn't mean to do it. I was so happy I didn't have to go to the doctor that I wasn't even upset with him. All was well.

Holidays at Our House

OUR HOUSE HUMMED with activity leading up to Christmas. By the middle of December the lists of gifts we wanted, in order of importance, had been written and checked twice; we were ready to begin our holiday preparations.

Two weeks before the big day, Mom and Kaye began making cookies and candy, which were off limits until Christmas morning. Pan after pan of peanut butter cookies, pecan crisps, chewy coconut squares, gingerbread men and sour-cream cookies filled the oven. We cut sugar cookies in the shapes of Christmas trees, stars and Santa Clauses that we decorated with colored powdered sugar. Mom also made the most delicious peanut brittle and chocolate fudge, which she put in decorative holiday tins and squirreled them away until just the right moment.

Kaye and Mom also worked on special sewing projects. One Christmas, they surprised the family with red corduroy, floor-length coachman robes. I don't know when they worked on the robes because none of us even had a hint of this special gift. I spent most of Christmas day in that robe. My mom was talented like that and sometimes made clothes for our dolls or knitted us sweaters.

My main task each season involved painting a Christmas scene on the living room windows, which because of the lights inside, could be seen by people as they walked or drove by our house. I usually chose a typical holiday setting to paint—shepherds, animals and the star shining on baby Jesus. I felt quite proud of my work and often went outside to gaze at the images illuminated by the soft, glowing light behind them.

During the week before Christmas, Dad began playing carols on the

MOM AND DAD ALL DRESSED UP

phonograph every evening. He carefully wiped the dust from the 33½ LPs and 45 records, and sounds of Bing Crosby, Mario Lanza, Nat King Cole and Perry Como filled our home. Over and over, we played "The Little Drummer Boy," "I'll Be Home for Christmas," "Ave Maria," and "White Christmas." Mom's routine involved lighting red and green candles, which smelled like cinnamon and evergreen trees. A couple of days before Christmas, Mom and Dad went into town and came home with a Scotch pine tied to the top of a taxi. We decorated our tree on Christmas Eve with colored lights, glass ornaments, silver icicles, and candy canes.

Dad had a job in a local bakery before he worked for the post office, so he knew how to bake. On Christmas Eve, he took over the kitchen, prepared dough for bread and cinnamon rolls and set it out to rise. It seemed like an eternity before his creations finally made it into the oven. Before we went to bed, he treated us to a slice of yeast bread, fresh from the oven, dripping with butter, but we had to wait for the morning to eat the cinnamon rolls.

Sometimes it was midnight before we finally put out milk and cookies for Santa and went to bed. Before falling asleep, I always sang a song to my baby sister Linda:

When I go to sleep
I never count sheep,
I count all the charms about Linda.

And lately it seems
in all of my dreams,
I walk with my arms about Linda.

I COULD NOT CARRY A TUNE, so Linda began singing the song to herself as soon as she could mouth the words. That took the fun out of it for me. My older sister Kaye read Christmas stories to us as we lay in bed, safe and secure in the knowledge that Santa was on his way with all the gifts we asked for, I hoped. "Kaye, do you think Santa will bring me what I want?"

"Well, have you been good, Jean?"

That wasn't what I wanted to hear. I tried again, "How about if I've been good most of the time?"

"If it wasn't too often," Kaye said in her authoritative way, "then maybe he might excuse those times when you were not-so-good."

I figured I'd take my chances. Maybe Santa didn't know about *all* the times I had been bad. Soon, I drifted off to sleep and dreamed about the horse and dog books, art supplies, horse statues, coloring books, paper dolls, and ice skates I wanted.

We awoke around 6:30 a.m. the next day, and at last, it was Christmas. Our morning routine was the same every year. We woke up early, put on our robes and went into the bathroom to brush our teeth and wash our faces. Then my parents forced us to sit on the top step of the stairs and *wait* while Daddy finished up in the bathroom. He did everything he could to draw out the time. He shaved in slow motion with a big grin on his face while we waited.

Finally after a half hour, which felt like ten hours, he stepped out of the bathroom and inched down the stairway. We sat and waited as he turned on the record player—always Bing Crosby:

I'm dreaming of a white Christmas
Just like the ones I used to know
Where the treetops glisten, and children listen
To hear sleigh bells in the snow

NEXT HE SAUNTERED OVER to the Christmas tree, turned on the lights, and called up to us "Okay, you can come down now." We jumped up, pushed and shoved our way down the stairs, each trying to be the first to get to the bottom. Once there, we sat in stunned silence at the beauty of the tree and all the colorfully wrapped presents beneath it. Mom avoided the stampede and came down the stairs carrying Linda a few minutes after we did.

Mom and Dad chose one of us each year to pass out the gifts, one present at a time, and we took our time opening each box. We received mostly clothes we needed, a few special gifts we asked Santa for, and books, always books—*Little Women* for Kaye, *The Hardy Boys* for Donnie, and *Lassie Come Home* for me. A book was a great gift. I loved holding a brand new book and enjoyed the slick feel of the dust jacket. I opened it and buried my face into the pages, smelling the freshly inked words on pages no one had ever read before. I usually finished the book before the day ended. I typically also received coloring books, watercolors, paper, clay, paper dolls—activities to keep me busy for hours on cold, winter days when going outside was not an option.

With all the presents opened and the wrapping paper cleaned up, we went into the kitchen where we feasted on Dad's cinnamon rolls while Mom fixed us a special Christmas breakfast of pancakes and bacon. Holiday music filled the house all day, and we enjoyed our gifts while snowflakes fell outside the windows and covered the frozen ground.

I REMEMBER ONLY ONE Christmas that wasn't so festive in our home. During the holidays that year, all of us kids came down with the stomach flu, so no one touched any of the cookies and candies we made. We came downstairs on Christmas morning, opened our presents and went back to bed for the rest of the day. On one of her many trips to the bathroom, Kaye didn't make it and vomited into the hot air register. Daddy removed the grate and cleaned it out as best he could, but that awful, sour smell overpowered the cinnamon rolls, the evergreen candles, and every other pleasant scent in our house that year.

MOM AND DAD attended many parties throughout the holiday season, but they did not often host these events, except for New Year's Eve. Even without looking at the calendar, I could tell when it was party time. Dad brought out his cigarette roller, tobacco and papers, and I rolled at least a hundred cigarettes for him. He put the liquor bottles at the end of the breakfast bar in the kitchen and placed the beer in the refrigerator. Next he retrieved a metal siphon, filled it with water, and put a soda charger on the top. When he squeezed the handle, soda water came out. Mom prepared platters of cheese, crackers, sour cream and onion dip, smoked oysters, deviled eggs, cookies, and cakes and spread them out on the dining room table. Once Dad had lined up the silly New Year's hats, everything was ready for the guests.

Dad answered the door chomping on a cigar, wearing a pair of black glasses that sported a huge nose and mustache that made him look like Groucho Marx. Without fail, everyone guffawed at the sight and just *had* to try on the ridiculous glasses. I watched this scene repeat throughout the night and thought about how silly adults were.

When it was time for us to go to bed, Kaye read us stories and nursery rhymes until she got tired and declared it was time for us to go to sleep. I lay in bed, listening to the muffled voices of everyone downstairs and drifted off. In my dream, I rode my trusty steed down the road. As I approached the town, I heard noisy conversation and loud laughter. My eyes shot open, and I realized I wasn't dreaming. The sound was coming from downstairs. *The party, oh yes, it was the darn party that woke me up.*

I hated to be awakened in the middle of the night. I lay there for a time, waiting for the noise to quiet down. It didn't. As the racket got louder and louder, I got madder and madder. Finally, I got out of bed, went down the hall and sat on the top step, contemplating my next move. *I'm going right down there and tell those people to shut up and go home. I hate you people!* I tried to build up my courage and go downstairs. Then I heard one of my parents' friends say, "Pearl, ya gotta listen to this song. I'll put it on the record player." Above all the other noise, I heard:

We've tried it once or twice
And found it rather nice

Roll me over lay me down and do it again
Roll me over in the clover, roll me over lay me down and do it again

Oh this is number one
And the fun has just begun

Roll me over lay me down and do it again
Roll me over in the clover, roll me over lay me down and do it again

"FRANNIE, TURN THAT DOWN. You're going to wake up the kids," Mom said. *Too late, Mom. I'm already up, and this kid is not happy!* I sat on that top step, miserable, cold and tired. Tears streamed down my cheeks, but I didn't have the nerve to go down there and tell them to get out of the house, so I could get some sleep. I wanted someone to notice me and ask what was wrong. That didn't happen. Finally, I gave up and went back to bed. After midnight, the crowd thinned out, and the noise level went down to only muffled sounds, so I eventually fell back asleep. I didn't say anything to my parents about how mad I was, but I never forgot that night.

Johnson Street School

THE SUMMER OF 1946 ended, and I started the sixth grade at Johnson Street School, located about a mile from my house. I usually walked or roller skated the fifteen or twenty minutes to school unless the weather was bad, and I had to take the bus. Sometimes I met up with friends—Gayle, Norma, Sherry or Janet—along the way, and we passed the time with all the usual chatter—what someone was wearing, who didn't get her homework done.

As soon as we arrived at the two-story, red-brick school, we went directly to our homeroom, finished up our homework, and waited for our teacher, Miss Thoreson, to come in and take attendance. Then we were off to our first class of the day.

Changing classrooms was a new experience for me. Until then, I had always stayed with the same teacher in the same room. Miss O'Neill was a tall, skinny, old woman—at least in her forties—with short, frizzy, brown hair, a receding chin, and glasses that sat on the end of a hooked nose. She reminded me of a turtle, all bent over with a long, scrawny neck.

Even though her hands were gnarled with arthritis, she used the long, pointed nail of her middle finger to bop us on the tops of our heads when we misbehaved, which was every day. I often had to stay after school for some misdeed—usually being sassy or talking when I shouldn't have been—but I knew that was the worst that could happen to me. The teachers paddled the boys but not the girls.

JEAN'S SIXTH-GRADE CLASS – JEAN SEATED, SECOND FROM RIGHT

WE HAD ALL STARTED TO MATURE, and suddenly members of the opposite sex were no longer *snots* or *brats;* they were sort of interesting. One day Clark decided to show off in front of us girls by walking on top of a metal, three-foot tall, round, pipe railing that bordered the sidewalk around the front of the school. Clark was a small, skinny, cocky kid who really liked the girls. He used the school steps to climb on top of the railing, holding onto the wall for balance.

Then Clark began to walk slowly down the metal pipe, one step, two steps, three steps...one foot in front of the other. I was transfixed; I couldn't take my eyes off him. Four steps, five, six and then...trouble. Clark started to teeter on the pipe. He flailed his arms in the air, desperately trying to recover his balance, but he knew this was not going to turn out well. Just then, his feet slipped out from under him, one on each side of the three-inch railing. He crashed down onto his crotch and rolled to the ground in a big ball. He had a wild look in his eyes and took in huge gasps of air but made no sound.

Clark could be annoying, but I felt sick just watching him in such pain. I just stood there with my mouth open; I didn't even think to go get help for him. Finally, Clark pulled himself up and looked all around, hoping not too many kids saw him. Then he limped off like a wounded animal.

ON OUR WAY TO SCHOOL one morning, Gayle, Norma, Sherry, Janet and I ran into Bobby and Dick. They were standing on the corner of Roy Street and Conewango Avenue, watching the girls while Dick made remarks as each passed by. As we approached, Dick looked at me and said, "Whadee ya say, four eyes?" I knew he was talking to me because I was the only girl wearing glasses. I glared at him and his scrawny body while he just stood there with his pinched nose and stupid grin on his pale face. "Hey, do you know you're a hermaphrodite?" Dick yelled to me. We just kept walking past them. I looked at Bobby who had sweet, brown eyes and a nice smile. He would never say anything like that to anyone and looked almost apologetic for his rude friend.

Out of earshot of the boys, I asked my friends, "Do you know what a *hermaphrodite* is? No one did. I decided to wait until I got home and ask Mom.

AFTER SCHOOL, I walked into the kitchen, slamming the door behind me, and dropped my book bag on the table. "Mom, where are you?"

"Up here, Jean," Mom yelled from the upstairs bedroom. "I'm putting clothes away."

I ran up the stairs to meet her. Once I caught my breath, I asked, "Mom, what's a *hermaphrodite?*"

"Well, Jean, it is someone that's part male and part female. Where did you hear that word?"

"You know that awful Richard Lundahl?" Mom nodded. "Well, on my way to school, I saw dumb old Richard, and he called me that. He also called me *four eyes!*"

"He's nothing but a little snot," Mom said, "That's what he is, and he's got no business calling you that. Don't pay any attention to him. He's got a lot of growing up to do."

A BOY AT JOHNSON STREET SCHOOL named Douglas had a crush on me. Douglas with his dishwater blond hair and pale blue eyes did not appeal to me at all. Every day when class let out, he waited for me and stared with that silly, puppy-dog look. He walked alongside me until he reached his house, one block from the school. I never liked him. He couldn't keep his fingers away from his nose and his mouth.

ONE DAY ON MY WAY home from school, I passed by the Children's Home on Conewango Avenue and Terrace Street and saw a little girl with her face pressed against the chain-link fence. The small, thin girl looked a few years younger than I did and was dressed in a pinafore, dark socks and scruffy brown shoes. Her pretty, light blue eyes peered out from under the bangs of a Dutch-boy haircut and focused on some faraway point.

"Hey, little girl, what's your name?"

"I'm Lily," she said in a voice so soft, I could barely make out the words.

"Why are you in there?"

"My mommy didn't have any money to keep me, so she brought me here. She promised she'd come back and get me soon."

"How long have you been here?"

"A couple of months, I guess. She'll be here soon. I know she will."

"My name's Jean, and I'll stop by to talk on my way home from school, if you're out here," I said and started my walk home.

I FOUND MY MOM in the kitchen, told her about the little girl I met and begged her to adopt Lily. Even before meeting Lily, I had been forever asking my parents to adopt a little girl. Every time I brought up the subject, Mom explained that we had enough children in our family, and we could not afford another one. But this time was different. Lily needed a good home and people to care about her. We *needed* to adopt her, but I could not convince my mother. I finally gave up and went upstairs to my books and drawing tablets. I thought about how sad Lily must feel being all alone.

I visited Lily a few more times on my way home from school, and then she wasn't at the fence anymore. Every day, I looked for her in the groups of kids playing in the compound, but I never saw her again. I hoped and prayed her mother had come for her and that she lived in a happy home with a family who loved her.

Innocence Was Bliss

THE SUMMER OF 1947 ended, and my world changed, seemingly overnight. In September, I started my seventh year of school at Beaty Junior High, a lifetime away from the familiar halls of the Home Street and Johnson Street schools where I had spent the last six years. Beaty sat on Third Street, more than a mile from my house; the Johnson Street School was only a block away from Beaty. It now took me a half hour to walk to school. I knew everyone in my elementary school, but now, kids from all over Warren assembled at Beaty to attend the seventh, eighth and ninth grades. Beaty had more teachers, more classes, more activities, and more stress, for me, at least.

I was twelve years old, and boys weren't just playmates anymore. I looked at them differently, in a way that I didn't quite understand. Instead of planning my next adventure, I pondered different things: *What should I wear? How do I look? Who is the new boy in class? How can I get that new pair of shoes? Maybe we will see the boys if we go to the movies on Saturday.*

Being popular became critically important. The school had a host of groups—the best dressed, smartest, most fun-loving, best looking, most athletic, and so forth. I was part of the most fun-loving group, and as a result of putting all my energy into having a good time, my grades plummeted. My older sister Kaye had almost perfect marks, and my brother Donnie's grades reflected the boredom he felt in school. Doing well in school just didn't seem important to me at that time, a problem from which I never quite recovered.

I MADE NEW FRIENDS at Beaty Junior High School. Patti Hesch and I hit it off right from the start. Patti was a thin, blue-eyed blonde with a bundle of energy, ready for anything, and a great sense of humor, which probably helped her survive as the youngest of five children. My father knew the Hesch family, and I learned that my mother's mother, Grandmother Ecklund, had been a wet nurse for Mr. Hesch's parents in the early 1900s.

I sometimes spent the night at Patti's house on the weekends. In the evenings, we did the usual kid things—lay on her bed and talked about clothes and boys, laughed hysterically over every little thing—but after her parents went to bed, we snuck out and went to the corner to hang out and smoke cigarettes. We finished off a pack of cigarettes in a half hour and then crept back into the house and went to bed.

Patti was Catholic, and before we could go to sleep, she had to recite the rosary. I helped her out by taking turns on all those Hail Marys:

Hail Mary, full of grace. Our Lord is with thee. Blessed art thou among women, and blessed is the fruit of thy womb, Jesus. Holy Mary, Mother of God, pray for us sinners, now and at the hour of our death.
Amen.

I DIDN'T UNDERSTAND why she had to say all those prayers every night, but if it helped her get into heaven, it was alright with me.

BETTE GAYLE SCALISE was another new friend I made in junior high. Bette was of Italian and Native American descent and had dark skin, short black hair, sparkling brown eyes and long eyelashes that she batted at all the boys. Her flirty, buoyant personality and crazy sense of humor kept us entertained during the long, boring school days.

Bette possessed a unique talent I could never successfully copy. When we sat next to each other in class, she nudged me and whispered, "Watch this" as she nodded to the boy in front of her on the next row. She opened her mouth slightly, curled her tongue, and used the tip to press down on a salivary gland. Immediately, a fine spray of spit flew across the room onto the back of the boy's neck. He grabbed his collar and looked up and all around to see where the water came from. Bette buried her head in her lesson and didn't look the least bit guilty.

As soon as the boy turned back to reading, she did it again, this time spraying his book. The unsuspecting boy spent most of the class trying to determine the source of the leak. He never once considered Bette as the culprit. The difficult part for us was not to burst out laughing as we watched that poor boy. I begged her to show me how to spray spit, and she tried. I just about crawled into her mouth, but I could never see how she did it.

WITH ALL MY NEW FRIENDS, schoolwork, shopping, listening to music, and these new boy-related adventures, I had little time to do the things I used to love like going fishing. One cool, windy fall morning, I decided to do something about that situation. I put on my jacket, grabbed my pole, whistled for Spot, and left for a day of fishing, with one small deviation. Since I was twelve now, I thought I'd buy a pack of Camels or Pall Malls to smoke while I fished; smoking cigarettes and fishing sounded like a mature thing to do. I made my purchase at Churchill's Grocery and headed for the *crick*.

I settled down on a nice, comfortable rock and used the half a loaf of bread I brought with me to make bread balls as bait. I took a slice of bread, tore off the crust, put a bit of water on the soft, white center and rolled it into a ball in the palms of my hands. Then I placed a bread ball on my hook, but as soon as I threw out my line, the bait went one way and the hook another. This was not going to help me catch the big carp I felt destined to bring home today. I tried a second bread ball, same results, just like my third, fourth and fifth tries. Finally, I took some extra fishing line and wrapped it around the bread ball on the hook, and that worked. I settled back onto the rock and waited for my amazing catch.

Now's a great time to have a cigarette. I took the pack out of my pocket, tore off a corner of the cellophane and foil at the top of the package and tapped out one of the twenty or so cigarettes inside. I had brought kitchen matches with me because I knew the breeze was too much for the little matches in a book. I lit the match on a rock and raised the flame to the cigarette in my mouth. *Whoosh!* The wind blew the flame into my face and caught my hair on fire. I heard the sizzle and smelled the stench of burning hair. I dropped the match, scooped up some dirt and threw it in my face to put out the blaze. Then I inhaled some of the dirt, resulting in a coughing fit. When the fire was out and I was able to breathe again, I brushed some of the dirt off my face and felt around to assess the damage. I could feel where my eyelashes and eyebrows *should* have been; now they were merely singed nubs. The hair around my face was burned as well. This was not going to be a good fishing day, so I picked up my gear and left for home, hoping to sneak in through the side door and run upstairs without anyone seeing me.

I was in luck. No one was around, so I raced to the upstairs bathroom. In the mirror, I saw the blackened face of someone with singed hair and only few eyelashes and eyebrows left, but thankfully my glasses would cover most of the damage. I washed my face, crinkled up my hair and went downstairs. No one noticed, not even my mom and dad. I didn't know whether to be grateful that I didn't get caught doing a foolish thing or upset because my parents didn't really look at me.

IN OCTOBER OF 1947, Gayle invited me and all of our friends, twelve or so boys and girls, to a Halloween party at her house. She decorated the basement with orange and black crepe paper and candles and had a record player blasting the music of Frankie Laine, Phil Harris, and Bing Crosby and a large aluminum washtub full of water and apples for dunking. In the doorway of the little room where she did the ironing, she hung a curtain to set it off from the rest of the party. Gayle informed us that this was the *kissing room* we would use while playing spin the bottle later in the evening. After we had our fill of potato chips and popcorn, Halloween cookies and sodas, and dunked for apples, it was time to play *the game*.

We sat in a large circle, all focused on the empty Coca-Cola bottle in the middle. We each took a turn, spinning the bottle and going into the little room to kiss the person the bottle pointed to when it finally came to rest. I had never kissed a boy before, so this was all new to me.

Everything went smoothly, and we all were having a great time until Norma spun the bottle, and it landed on Clark. We all loved Clark. He was cute with a nice personality and a sweet smile. Norma came out of the kissing booth, making a terrible face and said yuk to me under her breath. Gayle's spin picked out Clark as well, and she returned with a disgusted look on her face, like she had just eaten something terrible. "Okay, time out," all the girls said in unison. We stopped the game and huddled together.

"It's Clark," said Gayle. "Once he gets us back in the room, he grabs us real tight."

"Yeah," said Norma. "Then he opens his mouth real wide and sticks his tongue down your throat."

"That's disgusting," I said.

"He said his brother Bill showed him how to kiss girls," Gayle added.

"Maybe someone should show his brother how to kiss," Janet said.

We went back to the game, but when the bottle picked Clark, we all refused to go into the kissing room with him. The party broke up shortly after that, and we all went home. Spot was waiting for me on Gayle's front porch. "Let's go home, Spot. This learning how to kiss boys is stupid." We trudged home in the dark. I was already tired of this growing-up business.

Every day people do every day things
In every day places on every day strings
Oh to be different and do crazy things
In strange far off places on soft angel wings

Epilogue

YEARS PASSED and I returned to Warren to see what was left of my childhood stomping grounds and get together with some old school friends I hadn't seen in some time. In between those happy reunions, I traveled between the woods and the *crick*, as we called it, to see what was still there.

First, I went back to my house on Kenmore Street, which seemed small and old. The garage was so tiny; I don't know how I ever thought I could keep a horse in there, which was my plan. A back room had been added onto the house, and the four windows in the bathroom I almost burned up were still there.

I went down to the *crick*, the location of many of my adventures, and its size surprised me. The *crick* seemed much wider than I remembered. I don't know how I had the courage to cross it with my dog, Spot.

From the *crick*, I climbed back in the car and drove up Conewango Street, past the site where Churchill's Grocery once stood; the store had been turned into a house. I cruised in front of my friend Gayle's house and on up Quaker Hill Road, which was now paved. I looked to the left where our prairie had been; it was now covered with houses. I continued up the road to see if any part of the Fox Farm remained, but instead of the farm, I found another housing development.

I turned around and made my way up the Conewango Avenue extension to check out the dam, but nothing remained. I was told it had disintegrated several years earlier. The Colvins' old ramshackle house on Conewango was no more, now just a vacant lot. The Homestreet School was deserted. I passed by what once was The Children's Home, and in my mind's eye, I

THE CRICK

could still see Lily, peering through the chain link fence. I hoped she had been reunited with her mother and enjoyed a happy life. I was so disheartened when I drove down Second Avenue and saw my grandparents' old house. It was rundown and in desperate need of repairs. I couldn't find a trace of the magnificent old home it had once been.

REMINISCING AT THE CRICK

The next day I went to the Southside in search of the Lindsey Farm and its old barn with the rope swing. It was long gone; the land covered with houses. With a desperate need to see something familiar, I went to the Warren Library to look for Beatrice, the supposed goddess who lovingly watched over me in my grandparents' home. I found her in the genealogy section on one of the bookshelves, still looking as serene as ever.

While at the library, I inquired about the Warren State Hospital and one of the women knew Karen Ervin who was in charge of the medical library there. She kindly called her and made an appointment the next day to have her show me through the tunnels.

LOOKING AT
THE CHILDREN'S HOME

I had never been inside the State Hospital buildings, just the tunnels, when my partner, Bob and I entered the main building to meet Karen. The building was cavernous and gave me an eerie feeling when I opened the thick double front doors, leading to an ungodly long hallway. The arched hallway reached two stories high and was lined with closed offices on each side. The brightly colored drapes that covered the floor-to-ceiling office windows did little to combat the somber mood. Plus, there was not a person to be found anywhere.

We walked to the end of the hall to an office with a half-door where we signed in. We told the guard why we were there, and he called Karen Ervin. Within a few minutes, a frail, thin young woman in a colorless suit extended her hand to us. I had never experienced a handshake such as this. Karen's small hand was limp and cold, nearly devoid of life. It folded over in mine, like there was no strength in it at all. She seemed to fit into the atmosphere of the place.

Karen walked us to an elevator around the corner. When the doors opened, six or seven women stepped out, accompanied by a guard. Some looked at us warily; others simply held blank stares, focused on something from another realm.

I asked Karen if I could see the tunnels. She agreed to take us down but stated that I could not photograph the tunnels. We rode the same elevator a floor down from the main floor, and the door opened right into the tunnels. It was a lot like I remembered but even narrower and more oppressive. Karen stated that the employees used the tunnels sometimes to take shortcuts to different parts of the buildings, but all doors to the outside had been closed permanently. We looked around for a bit but soon got claustrophobic and decided we'd seen enough.

I didn't see the rooms of mattresses, office furniture, and appliances and wasn't quite sure what was behind some of the doors. We thanked Karen for her time and went back to the guard's station to sign out. When I mentioned where we'd been, he said most people didn't know it, but there were tunnels below the tunnels. He had just been down there a week before and saw some old office furniture. Were those the tunnels we played in as children? Did we go somewhere most people didn't even know about?

MY DOG SPOT DIED at age twelve from cancer. She was my faithful friend to the end and the smartest dog I ever had.

I finally did get my own horse when I was thirty nine years old. I saw an ad in the newspaper: *black two-year-old, green-broke Anglo Arab gelding for sale: $200.* I could hardly contain my excitement when I called and found out he was still for sale. He was beautiful, shiny-black and spirited, and if I bought him, I could rent a stall only a few miles from my apartment. It would be no trouble to take care of him every day. I had several wonderful years with Setcha, riding him out in the woods and fields in Palm Beach Gardens, Florida until I sold him. I understand he became a jumper. My next horse was a thirteen-year-old registered palomino Paso Fino stallion called Rico di Oro. He was beautiful under saddle and pure pleasure to ride, never requiring more than a light rein. Always a Don Juan with the mares, Rico pranced and danced around until they noticed him. I rode him at my home in Jupiter Farms, Florida along the dirt roads and in the fields in that area for many, years.

I finally achieved my dream of having my own horses and what a great dream it was!

About
Jean L. DeLong

BORN IN WARREN, Pennsylvania at the end of the Great Depression, just before the outbreak of World War II, Jean DeLong grew up with a hunger for adventure and continued her quest when she moved to Florida in 1966. Her many passions include writing her childhood memories, art and photography as well as living life to the fullest with her partner Bob and faithful companions, Jack and Dyna—short for Crackerjack and Dyna-Mite.

Born 7/06/1935—

CPSIA information can be obtained
at www.ICGtesting.com
Printed in the USA
FFHW010213051218
49708738-54145FF